Gods and Planets

THE ARCHETYPES OF ASTROLOGY

Ellynor Barz

Gods and Planets

THE ARCHETYPES OF ASTROLOGY

translated by Boris Matthews

Chiron Publications   ★   Wilmette, Illinois

Editor's Note: The dates assigned to the zodiac throughout are those that were used in the original German edition. These dates vary slightly from year to year, however, and exact dates for a given year can be found in a comprehensive horoscope book.

Originally published in 1988 as *Götter und Planeten: Grundlagen archetypischer Astrologie.* Copyright 1988, Kreuz Verlag.

Translation © 1991 by Chiron Publications.

All illustrations (except for diagrams) are taken from Heinz Artur Strauss, *Der astrologische Gedanke in der deutschen Vergangenheit,* (Munich, 1926).

Library of Congress Catalog Card Number: 93-17281

Printed in the United States of America.
Copyediting and book design by Siobhan Drummond.
Cover design by D. J. Hyde

Library of Congress Cataloging-in-Publication Data:

Barz, Ellynor, 1931–
   [Götter und Planeten. English]
   Gods and planets : the archetypes of astrology / Ellynor Barz :
translated by Boris Matthews.
    p. cm.
   Translation of: Götter und Planeten.
   Includes bibliographical references.
   ISBN 0-933029-71-3 : $16.95
   1. Astrology and mythology. 2. Astrology and psychology.
3. Archetype (Psychology)—Miscellanea. I. Title.
BF1729.M9B37 1993
133.5'3—dc20   93-17281
                                                 CIP

ISBN 0-933029-71-3

Contents

Foreword **vii**
Introduction **ix**

I. The Planets 1
The Gods: In the Beginning Was the Story ✶ *Myths Are Images of Powers in the Soul* ✶ *Astrological Interpretation*

Myths of the Beginnings 9
Uranus ✶ *Kronos (Saturn)* ✶ *Zeus (Jupiter)* ✶ *Poseidon (Neptune)* ✶ *Hades (Pluto)* ✶ *The Psychological Views of Creation Myths*

Jupiter (Zeus): New World Order 32
Jupiter as Origin and Possibility ✶ *Ares (Mars)* ✶ *Aphrodite (Venus)* ✶ *Hermes (Mercury)*

Sun and Moon 62
The Moon ✶ *The Sun*

II. The Zodiac 85
The Zodiac the Sun, and Precession

The Signs of the Zodiac 95
Aries ✶ *Taurus* ✶ *Gemini* ✶ *Leo* ✶ *Virgo* ✶ *Libra* ✶ *Scorpio* ✶ *Sagittarius* ✶ *Capricorn* ✶ *Aquarius* ✶ *Pisces*

III. The Houses 147
I. House *Vita* ✶ II. House *Lucrum* ✶ III. House *Fratres* ✶ IV. House *Genitor* ✶ V. House *Filii* ✶ VI. House *Valetudo* ✶ VII. House *Nuptiae* ✶ VIII. House *Mors* ✶ IX. House *Pietas* ✶ X. House *Honores* ✶ XI. House *Amici* ✶ XII. House *Inimica*

IV. Quadrants, Elements, Pairs of Opposites, Aspects 175
Quadrants ✶ *Elements* ✶ *Pairs of Opposites* ✶ *Aspects*

Conclusion 186

Notes **188**
Bibliography **191**

Foreword

This book deals with basic concepts of astrology but is not a text-book.

It neither gives instructions for calculating horoscopes nor for systematically "interpreting" them but intends above all to assist the reader in recognizing the planets, the signs of the zodiac, and the houses, and thereby facilitates an "archetypal" understanding of astrology.

This book is directed to the astrological layman, but it may also suggest to the astrologer a little-known way of viewing astrology, and it might grant the interested psychologist access to a domain of knowledge and experience that is intimately related to psychology in a deeper sense than one might expect on the basis of a purely typological and diagnostic use of astrology.

My starting point is C. G. Jung's analytical psychology, which regards the soul as a dynamic whole consisting of conscious and unconscious aspects. There are profound correspondences between Jung's scientific discoveries and the empirical symbolic cosmos of astrology. Astrology itself is not a science, and in my opinion it should never make any claim to be; I have made several references to the scientific, *astronomical* facts that provide the foundation for astrology.

In retelling the old symbolic stories that underlie all astrological notions, I hope to contribute to an understanding of astrology that is not distorted by pseudoscientific pretensions but rather to one that recalls and ponders the analogies that have been perceived since time immemorial between the stars "out there" in the universe and the dynamic structures "within" our souls.

I would like to thank Fr. Sigrid Strauss-Kloebe, who was my teacher in astrology and likewise an analytical psychologist.

Introduction

In this chapter certain fundamental ideas will be introduced and several concepts clarified. The impatient reader who would like to skip the introduction should read at least the passages about the concepts of the symbol and projection in order not to approach the text entirely unprepared, having in mind a different understanding of these concepts than the one intended, since they are not explained elsewhere.

It is erroneous to believe that astrology exists as a clearly delineated, intellectual edifice or area of knowledge. This is not the case not only because astrology was banished from public consciousness for centuries, but also because it has to do with the "cosmic conditionality of the psyche" (Strauss-Kloebe 1968), with certain aspects of the human being in regard to which there are no definitive pronouncements.

Depending on the epoch (and the culture), the images of humankind and of the human soul change, as the various philosophical trends and, more recently, the various psychological schools show.

There never has been a unified body of astrological knowledge; today that is the case more than ever before. There has always been only the astrology of the astrologer with his or her personal background, his or her personal character. As a consequence of the purely rational direction of science in our times, today people in astrology generally still try to follow the approach of the natural sciences and to count astrology among the "objective" sciences. Psychology, too, when it is included among the sciences, is usually only accepted if it is a psychology of consciousness and thus, so to speak, the opposite of depth psychology, which addresses itself precisely to the unconscious parts of the psyche.

In this book I am not aiming for scientific observation. But I will refer to certain interrelationships in which I see the basis for a possible scientific approach to astrology.

It is now widely accepted in the domain of scientific observation that what is observed includes the observer, that the notion of a "clean" separation of subject from object is an illusion, that "objective" observation is not possible in the sense once postulated, indeed, that the observer and the observed coincide. And this is most certainly true when the observed and the observer are of the same nature.

Jungian psychology—and modern physics—have created new conditions for a renewed, wholistic view of the world in which the external world and the inner world of the soul are no longer seen as fundamentally separated from one another.

In this context it has become possible to approach astrology with fewer reservations, and by virtue of this, astrology gains a new power to attract in that it approaches a wholistic understanding of humankind and the world.

We live in a time of transition from causal-mechanistic thought to a view that is again wholistic. In scientific observation up until now, the world—i.e., the observer and likewise the object of observation—was dissected into its basic components, components which were linked with each other in a "mechanical" causal relationship, which were separated in space, and which differed from each other. Since Einstein's discovery of the theory of relativity, the relativity of space and time has entered our consciousness.[1] Knowledge of his quantum theory—that both matter and energy have a double character as continuous waves or discrete particles—has fundamental implications not only for physics but likewise for psychology. Gradually these insights have also penetrated public consciousness. Popular publications of modern physicists have achieved an astonishing circulation; there is obviously a need for a new worldview.[2] At least there is a receptivity to one, since the preceding, one-sidedly rational development has led to overly technologized ways of living that are perfectly organized in every detail but devoid of meaning.

Modern physics has again made possible a wholistic, organic worldview: the notion of the universe as an unbroken whole in flowing movement. All parts are joined by indivisible links so that ultimately it is impossible to fragment the world into parts existing independently of each other.

The whole and its parts are mutually necessary categories and each implies the other. Every human being is not only a self-contained creature but also bound to the whole, including nature and the rest of humankind. This does not question the significance of the individual; every "part," each element of the whole, is in itself a relatively stable, autonomous, independent "whole" (Bohm, in Kakuska 1984).

These findings of modern physics are in agreement with the ideas of C. G. Jung, who in 1950 wrote about the complementary relationship between psychology and atomic physics and spoke about the interface between the psychic realm (the archetypal structures of the unconscious psyche) and the physical domain (1972, p. 176). He was of the opinion that a universal—divine—principle could be rediscovered even in the most minute part and that consequently even the smallest part was in agreement with and participated in the whole (1952, par. 924).

The principle of analogy states: "By virtue of his microcosmic nature, man is a son of the firmament or macrocosm . . . . Here the great principle or beginning, heaven, is infused into man the microcosm, who reflects the star-like natures and thus, as the smallest part and end of the work of Creation, contains the whole . . . . Expressed in modern language, the microcosm which contains 'the images of all creation' would be the collective unconscious" (Jung 1952, pars. 929, 926, 931).

Jung sees the collective unconscious as the foundation—the fundamental human psychic endowment and precondition—containing the fundamental (abstract) structures for all the possibilities of human experiencing. The archetypes of the collective unconscious are the form-giving patterns or structures in the human psyche. We humans can become conscious of them only by "seeing" them in images and experiences outside of ourselves. The collective unconscious is the totality of all possible psychic structures in humankind. But every individual likewise contains the collective unconscious: a part and yet the whole, in flowing movement.

Here there is a close connection with Johannes Kepler, the great astronomer and astrologer of the sixteenth and seventeenth centuries. Kepler summarized his insights in his magnum opus, *Harmonices Mundi* (The Harmony of the World). Corresponding to the harmonic structures of the universe, he saw in humankind an inherent structure that he called the "geometric instinct in man."[3] This instinct enabled human beings also to perceive the geometric structures of the outer world, and even those of the universe, and to "respond" to them in analogies.

Kepler was of the opinion that the stars exert an influence on human beings thanks to their emitting light, to geometry, and to the geometrically changing figures that they create among themselves. But above all, he saw the corresponding formative power in human beings, that very same "geometric instinct," through which "the soul responds to the geometric constellations" and gives them form in life. "The soul begins to dance in response to the enticement of the universe" (Strauss and Strauss-Kloebe 1981). The ear can hear the harmonies; the eye cannot see the geometries but can, in analogy to recognizing the harmonies, recognize them.[4]

Movement and rhythm—so we learn again from modern physicists—are essential characteristics of matter. Kepler arrived

Instruction in Astronomy
From the Lucidarius *(Augsburg, 1479)*

at the same insight on the basis of observing the "solid" heavenly bodies, the planets. And both Kepler and Jung—as well as modern physicists—saw in human beings corresponding structures that enable humankind to be cognizant of these interconnections; analogies in the psyche to the structures of the outer world, the cosmos, analogies between the whole and the part.

Against the background of these sorts of interconnections, Jung said, "Astrology consists of symbolic configurations, just as does the collective unconscious, with which psychology [his psychology!] is concerned: the planets are the 'gods,' symbols of the powers of the unconscious" (1972, p. 400).

Here we must turn our attention more penetratingly to the concept of the symbol, since understanding the symbol is a fundamental precondition for understanding the traditional content of astrology and "correctly" relating to it.

Among astrologers today, it is generally agreed that astrology is to be understood symbolically, and by this they mean "in an extended sense."

In the general understanding of symbols we again encounter two fundamentally different views of the world.

One group uses the symbol as metaphor: as an image for a certain abstract, rational concept. From this group we often hear expressions like "We must understand that symbolically" or

"We have to take that as a symbol," and this means only as a sign for something that could be expressed rationally just as well or even better. According to this view, symbolic thought as prerational thinking belongs to an early stage of human development. In the causal-mechanistic worldview of astrologers of this cast, symbolic ciphers are still utilized because they are part of astrological tradition.

A different point of view holds that the symbol represents a power that exceeds the rational consciousness of humankind and cannot be grasped causally. This concept of the symbol is, for all practical purposes, lost to contemporary usage, along with the wholistic worldview to which it belongs. This usage must appear suspect to a concretistic and deterministic worldview. With a wholistic view now possible once more, the concept of the symbol has attained a new meaning, and not only in depth psychology. For example, it occupies a central position in the work of theologian and philosopher of religion Paul Tillich, whose argument I follow in the subsequent reflections, which also take into consideration the astrological context.

Tillich identifies five characteristics of the symbol:

1. A symbol is plastic; it has a form perceptible to the senses; it points beyond itself. It is itself not the thing meant but points to something that cannot be grasped immediately or not as a whole, to something that, at the moment, exceeds comprehension.

This characteristic always holds true for astrological symbols, planets, signs of the zodiac, etc. They are phenomena in the heavens perceptible to the senses, and in them we experience more than planetary laws, more than causal realities; we experience our condition of subjection to something transcending the human being.

2. Taken by itself, the symbol is of no significance; rather, it participates in the reality of that to which it points.

Taken by itself, a symbol—for example, a number of stars that, with good will, we could take to represent a bull—is not yet of any significance. Only the return of various constellations at specified times and places and the experience of certain qualities of light or warmth and cold—and this within a reliable cycle year after year—permits us to intuit cosmic interconnections that transcend us human beings.

3. Symbols cannot be arbitrarily invented because they are not subject to expediency or convention. They are born and die, to speak graphically.

Cosmic powers, Moon, Sun, stars, all are experienced as numinous and therefore conceived of as divine figures. The names have changed; the powers remain alive and hence the symbols representing them—in Egypt, Babylon, Greece, and in the Christian domain, too—cling tenaciously to life. For most people, they are now dead; from "modern" astrologers we hear that modern astrology has only the names in common with the old planetary gods.

4. Through the power of the symbol, dimensions of reality are disclosed "that are usually concealed by the predominance of other dimensions. But the human spirit could not comprehend these new dimensions if the symbol did not simultaneously open up a new dimension in him" (Tillich 1964, p. 238).

Religious symbols, for example, mediate the experience of the sacred by their participation in the sacred. Encounters with sacred places, times, and images enable the individual to experience something of the sacred. And neither symbol nor religious experience can be rendered adequately in abstract terms.

A symbol is an archetypal image that represents one facet of that which itself gives form and shape. It works because it strikes corresponding structures in us humans, our "geometric instinct."

5. The fifth feature is the constructive ordering and the disintegrative destructive power of the symbol. In general, we think only of its stabilizing, indeed healing, power. But it takes both sides to make a whole.

Hence, we will find both aspects in each astrological symbol. And the horoscope as a whole contains "harmonious" stabilizing and "unharmonious" disruptive aspects.

The positive or negative effect of a symbol depends, on the one hand, on the nature of that toward which the symbol points and, on the other, on the spirit in which we understand and encounter it.

Taken in this sense, the myths of the planetary gods presented in the next chapter are symbols. The myth, like the symbol, is a self-contained form that cannot be reduced or dissolved. In the myth, there is no distinction between part and whole. Each myth is a totality and, simultaneously, a part of a totality. The parts do not exist in and of themselves but rather are ordered about a center from which they gain their form and their meaning. Likewise myths, viewed intrapsychically, are parts of the soul as a whole, which potentially always embraces them. We can just as well regard myths as projections of the unconscious psyche, the collective unconscious.

Here we must pause to consider the concept of *projection* in order to understand how we can see myths or symbols as projections of unconscious psychic contents.

> Considered psychologically, symbols are the result of projections of unconscious contents to external objects that, either as a whole or thanks to certain of their component parts, are suitable vehicles for the projections. By the term *projection* we understand an emotional process taking place unconsciously that consists in this: a part or a content of the soul or psyche not directly perceptible to consciousness—hence something nonmaterial—is externalized and thus projected to a concrete object, like a film projected on a screen. In the view of Jungian psychology, this process carries an overarching significance, for in this view unconscious contents become accessible to consciousness exclusively via projection, except by way of feelings and intuition, which remain incomprehensible to a great extent. To make it graphic, one could say quite simply: since consciousness cannot see into its unconscious inner realm, it depends on emanations and on their striking a suitable surface; only then does consciousness see on this surface, on the carrier of the projection, a likeness of what originates from its inaccessible interior. (Barz 1979, p. 87f)

Not until projected onto the screen of life, or of the heavens, do we meet the inner powers as symbols outside of ourselves, and these symbols can have so strong a force to affect us because we relate them to the energies of our unconscious potential.

In this sense, our entire experience of the world can be called a projection.

We human beings can relate to the world of projections or of symbols in many different ways. We can be completely consumed by the world of outer phenomena, be joined with them in profound unconsciousness, and feel ourselves handed over to them as though to good or evil powers. Then we experience ourselves as conditioned or dependent on the outer world; but, viewed in the perspective of depth psychology, we are conditioned by unconscious contents in ourselves that we project outward. When this happens, it can be a question, speaking astrologically, of the various planetary forces, or of other contents, that affect us as structures or gods. But we ourselves must recognize them as parts of our own inner world.

Again and again in the course of our life, it is a question of becoming conscious, and that means recognizing projections and withdrawing them or taking back what we first *had to* project to the external world in order to see it at all. Thus it is again a question of the relationship of the part to the whole; this time of our relationship to our surroundings.

Contents especially suited to being projected are so-called shadow aspects of ourselves, sides of ourselves that we don't want to see, even when we can see them. We project them to our fellows and battle them there. It is for us, as for the others, a necessary and important step eventually to recognize and accept these projections as parts of ourselves.

To this extent, we come to terms with psychic material without costing us our relationship to reality; rather, it can directly serve us in doing justice to reality. We take pains to see ourselves and our fellows "more objectively," not covering up others with projections and not maintaining an idealized image of ourselves.

Above and beyond that, every event of reality has reference to one's own psyche. I feel myself responsible for the reality outside me because I affect it, because I have a part in it; I, as a part, cannot separate myself from the whole.

Outer and inner world are mirrored in the horoscope. Cosmic factors are reflected in it, as are collective human experiences. In the astrological symbols we meet projections of the collective unconscious. In that each one of us, with a personal horoscope, participates in the fundamental astrological patterns of all, we cannot avoid our role as part of the whole. On the other hand, as individuals we cannot overlook the responsibility for the whole that falls to our lot as part of the whole: for the world surrounding us as well as for the people with whom we live.

Thanks to the personal horoscope, each of us is an irreplaceable individual, something indivisible, even when we consider the aspects and functions of the horoscope one at a time in order to understand them better.

We can look at the personal horoscope as an individual symbol which contains more of the individual than we can grasp at once, or ever: graphic, material, perceptible, but pointing to greater contexts and powers.

We could compare the horoscope to a dream. The individual elements of the dream—stairs, mountain, house, woman—are images we all know, that all of us can dream. In this sense, they are collective symbols. But as images in *my* dream, brought together in this unique constellation by my unconscious, they are—and the dream is—an individual symbol and therefore can be interpreted "correctly" only in conjunction with me.

In a manner of speaking, the personal horoscope represents an individual's personal equation. Jung says, "It seems as though the horoscope corresponds to a certain moment in the conversation of the gods, i.e., the archetypes of the psyche" (1972, p. 401).

This is an apt image for the constellation, the position of the planets vis-à-vis each other, at the moment of birth. By contrast, it would be an error were we to assume that this constellation says anything about the "content" of the conversation. To fathom that, we have need, as Jung says, of "both arts"—astrology and depth psychology—and above all of lived life: the individual's "response" to the fundamental pattern inherent in himself or herself.

I

The Planets

*The seven planets with their signs and their children and
their days of the week. The center is an aspect diagram.
Ca. 1490.*

The planets have always assumed the first place among all the phenomena comprising the panorama of the heavens. The seemingly self-willed moving stars—the planets, which alter their light and their speed of movement, which accelerate, halt, or even move backwards as seen from the vantage point of the observer, only to continue on their course anew—have called forth humankind's special notice and have always enticed us to respond. The names that the planets received attest to the significance attributed to them: they carry the names of the gods.

Originally there were only the figures of the gods and the myths that told of their origins and their doings. Toward the end of the sixth century B.C.E. the planets were assigned to the gods as their symbols, their representatives, so to speak. This took place independently of astrology or horoscopes. Nor were the planets identical with the gods. The planets were called "Star of Zeus," "Star of Aries," "Star of Aphrodite"—and later in the Roman Empire "Star of Jupiter," "Star of Mars," "Star of Venus"—until they received their own names later as independent powers, being understood differently (Boll, Gezold and Gundel 1977).

Later the fixed stars were also united in groups and named. But they assumed a lesser rank: the world of the heroes was assigned to them. They were reminders of the ancient legends or, as the people of those times experienced them, heroes who

3

had been rescued—or banished—by the gods to the heavens. But they now no longer had any life of their own as did the movable fixed stars (the planets) among them. There was—and still is— Perseus, Andromeda, Hercules, the Great Bear, Lyra (the lyre), the crown, Cygnus (the swan), the dolphin, Leo (the lion), Cancer (the crab), and many others. This imparted a special significance to those constellations through which the course of the sun and the other planets runs. The signs of the zodiac we know today still bear those names.

The Gods: In the Beginning Was the Story

Myths are stories of the gods in which a series of symbols are linked together into a whole.

Hesiod and Homer were the first poets (ca. 700 B.C.E.) known to compile the histories of the Greek gods. In his *Theogony*, Hesiod described the origin of the world and the birth of the gods. Homer celebrated the life of the gods and their appearance among human beings.

These works are not concerned with personal destinies; they are not individual poems. Rather, they are documents of religious emotion, and when they were written down, the gods were invoked. Homer and Hesiod recorded the stories that existed in many places and with many variations in an archetypal and generally valid form.

A myth is always a totality. It is timeless. The events take place in a time that is just as much "then" as "now." Nor is a myth bound to a specific locality. The locus of the story is in us.[5] Reflections of primordial forms of human experiencing are found in myths. They are not invented, but experienced.

What was inherent in the human soul was perceived "out there." From our contemporary point of view, we could say that the gods—on Olympus and in the world—were the result of projections of the human soul.

"It is a well-observed fact that we do not make projections but that they happen to us. This fact leads to the inference that we have derived our first psychological knowledge from the stars. That is to say, the closest from what is farthest away. In a certain sense, we have recollected ourselves from the universe" (Jung 1972, p. 309).

Humankind first experiences the abundance of phenomena externally. We cannot perceive the abundance in our souls if we have not first projected it into the external world so that it becomes visible. The soul is able to recognize analogies to its most intimate contents in distant things because they are inherent in the soul.

> *Were not the eye like to the sun*
> *The sun it never would perceive;*
> *Lay God's own power not in us,*
> *How ever could the Divine enchant us?*
> *(Goethe 1950, p. 629)*

But so that it can grasp the most distant things, the human spirit gives them human form: for example, the gods take on shapes resembling humans.

Myths Are Images of Powers in the Soul

Reflective consciousness is necessary for recognizing and interpreting constellations and experiences of the external world as projections of intrapsychic powers.

At first, there is always the spontaneous projection to a screen lying outside ourselves. Only later do we suspect and ultimately perceive the projection as such; and then—as far as consciousness is capable—we withdraw the projection, i.e., we recognize that what we experienced outside arises from the play of forces within us, and that inside and outside coincide, that we are perceiving both simultaneously.

Paracelsus (1493–1541) concluded that the perception of celestial phenomena was to be understood as analogous to the constellations in the human being, that we were dealing with primordial images in the human soul. He said that a physician ought to know "that the sun, moon, Saturn, Mars, Mercury, Venus and the signs of the zodiac are in man" (cited in Strauss-Kloebe 1934, p. 418).

Today it is analytical psychology, for example, that is concerned with comprehending these sorts of interrelationships. Hence, Jung regards the configurations in the collective unconscious as parallel to astrological observations: "The planets are the 'gods,' symbols of the powers of the unconscious" (1972, p. 401).

These powers are still living symbols—at least in astrology. This is demonstrated, among other things, by the fact that their names still live, even after the gods and their myths have disappeared from the consciousness of most people.

The planets are still designated by the Latin names of the Greek gods: Mercury is Hermes; Venus is Aphrodite; Mars is Ares, Jupiter is Zeus; Saturn is Kronos; Uranus has always been Uranus; Neptune was Poseidon; Pluto and Hades are the same.

It is noteworthy that astronomers, following the ancient tradition, gave Greek names to the three most recently discovered planets—Uranus (1781), Neptune (1846), and Pluto (1930)—and these names make sense mythologically, as we shall see. (The attempt to name Uranus for its discoverer, Herschel, was unsuccessful.)

In the fourth, eighth, and seventeenth centuries, an attempt was made "to Christianize the heathen firmament" (Sfountouris n.d., p. 80). But the old symbols in the domain of astrology were still so much alive that they could not be replaced by allegories or other names. For example, the attempt failed to replace the names of the twelve signs of the zodiac with the names of the twelve apostles. Even today they are so alive that they resist replacement even by psychological terms. The name *Saturn*, for example, is more embracing, has more layers of meaning, and is more effectual than all the expressions that might replace it or are associated with it.

Astrological Interpretation

When we make astrological interpretations, we face the challenge of bringing together the graphic symbols as well as the recognized, underlying psychic structures. The regularities that result serve as the foundation for astrological interpretation. Here, the path leads from the concretely visible to the general, from the image to the abstraction.

Even in astrology, the symbolic figure, the intuitive image, was originally intended. Now we refer more to the dynamics that find expression in the symbol. But these dynamics also correspond to archetypal functions. Even from the dynamics—the various tendencies of the individual planets to move this way or that—we deduce primordial patterns, analogous to the graphic myths (rapid Mars; slow, restrictive Saturn).

It is important that we remain aware of the analogies to the movements or the parallelism of events that are not based upon causality. Concurrently seeing both inner and outer is possible on the basis of synchronicity, but not of causality. This signifies the rejuvenation of an older point of view at a higher level of consciousness.

The danger of relapsing into causal thinking remains, for example, suddenly interpreting generally ascertained regularities on a personal level and relating them causally to biographical events.

It seems as though the horoscope corresponds to a certain moment in the conversation of the gods, i.e, to the archetypes of the psyche. Gaining access to the conversation would mean making the natal horoscope into specific, biographical facts.

But pondering or interpreting the natal chart can only be a question of establishing a general, fundamental structure of the psychic layout. Only the individual can relate the specific content, the biographical detail to his or her natal horoscope. Hence, we do not introduce anything foreign into the interpretation of the horoscope; rather, we open our eyes to the structures in the individual's life pattern that, at specific times and on various levels, can manifest concretely in very diverse ways.

The planets are "gods," the archetypes of the unconscious. We must not yield to the illusion that an archetype can finally be explained and thus gotten rid of or be translated into something else. "Even the best attempt at explanation is merely a more or less fortunate translation into another metaphorical language" (Jung).

The more we comprehend the way archetypal dynamics present themselves—that is, the greater the extent to which the primordial archetypal image as the underlying pattern is carried over into our understanding—the more readily can we recognize ourselves and our own patterns of experience in it. Then I can ask myself: How do these patterns take on concrete expression in my life? How do I behave then? What other possibilities are there for me to live in accordance with my basic pattern and perhaps to act more meaningfully or more adequately?

Every planet in the horoscope unites polarities within itself and "provokes an answer" (Kepler) ·in one direction or another. It represents a comprehensive whole and is, at the same time, a part of a supraordinate totality, of the cosmos without and within, graphically depicted in the horoscope.

The cooperation or opposition of the gods or planets graphically mirrors the possible interplay of forces and potentialities in us. The outcome of every "interplay" will be different, depending on how the forces and powers relate to one another and how we meet them.

Myths of the Beginnings

In the beginning, cosmic order crystallized only gradually from the original chaos. The Greek myths of the origin of the world are concerned with battles among the various generations of the gods, but likewise with battles between heaven and earth, and earth and the abyss, in which powers from all the realms—the upper and the lower—are involved.[6] The theater of the development is Gaia, the earth. She is both the one affected as well as an active participant, until her domain is finally so well staked out that concrete history can begin there.

It would be wrong to see this process only in a chronological sense as the development of humanity or as a developmental history. These "stories" or processes take place in each human being anew, but they unfold not only chronologically, not only linearly. In the individual, there is a point when consciousness begins to develop; the individual develops over time, has a life history; and concurrently all the "gods," all the archetypes, are always synchronically "at work" in us, as—reflected in the horoscope—they manifest their effects in us as functions or press for actualization from the beginning to the end of our life. Again and again Uranus breaks through; ever and again we feel Pluto's threat; again and again we experience the weight of Saturn's hand or the confusion and illusion Neptune sows; and in us is also Jupiter who creates order—all as intrapsychic functions.

The planetary gods *distant* from the earth, and the principles manifesting through them, we sense more in the background or "underground." Those *near* the earth determine life that is accessible to consciousness; they shape the experiences and patterns of behavior we perceive in daily life.

In my discussion, I will first recount the stories of the gods whose names the planets bear. Then I will take up the intrapsychic powers that these stories reflect, the psychic structures that underlie them. Finally, I will build a bridge to interpreting the planetary gods in astrology.

When asked what the planetary symbols mean in the horoscope, I relate them to areas of individual psychic experience. In this context, I usually no longer speak expressly of symbols or functions or principles, but simply name the names, for example, Uranus or Saturn. This sounds like an oversimplification and a personalization. But actually I have in mind the entire range and extent of the qualities belonging to the planetary symbol, the whole field of forces it designates.

In the myths, I will use the Greek names of the gods; when speaking astrologically or psychologically, the Latin names, as is customary.

I will begin with myths of the beginnings and relate them up to the point when Zeus divided up the world. Then I will consider what the symbols of Uranus, Saturn, Jupiter, Neptune, and Pluto are intended to express psychologically and astrologically before I describe, in a second section, how, so to speak, under Jupiter's rule the division of our world into various domains began; how psychic life became differentiated and manifested in the spectrum of the planets near the earth.

In the case of each planet, myths that tell of the planetary god shall be the basis for our attempt, first, to understand that god as an intrapsychic power or function and, second, arrive at the god's astrological interpretation. Often the transitions will be fluid because psychological and astrological observations can seldom be precisely delimited but tend to complement each other organically.

The Sun and the Moon conclude the series. These two greatest heavenly luminosities—as seen from the earth—are for us the most moving, but also those closest to consciousness. It seemed to make sense to put them at the conclusion and thereby give them a more prominent place. However, my discussion of the Sun will be much less extensive than that of the Moon, because

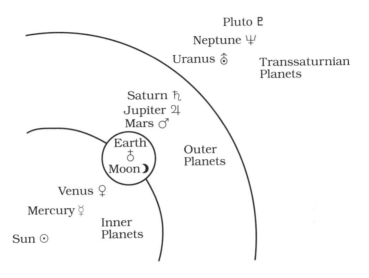

Diagram of the Planetary System (Heliocentric)
From Ernst von Xylander, Lehrgang der Astrologie, *p. 113*

the following chapter on the signs of the zodiac presents a further elaboration of the symbol of the Sun.

A dream accompanies consideration of each planet. They are my dreams; I dreamt them during the time I was concerned with just these chapters, and hopefully they will show how close together astrological themes and the psychological actually do lie.

Uranus

According to Hesiod, in the beginning only Chaos, the yawning abyss, existed (and Eros, the cosmogonic principle of creation, as a primordial potency). Out of Chaos arose Gaia, "of the broad breast" (*Theogony* 117). She gave birth to the mountains and the unfruitful, desolate sea. Then she created from within herself "one who matched her every dimension, Uranus, the starry sky, to cover her all over" (*Theogony* 126–127).

Now there were Heaven and Earth, something masculine and something feminine, yang and yin. They united in cosmic *hieros gamos*. Uranus "came on bringing night with him, and desiring love he embraced Gaia and lay over her stretched out complete" (*Theogony* 176–178).

11

Thereupon Gaia bore six daughters and six sons, the Titans. The youngest was Kronos (Saturn), the strongest of her sons. But she also gave birth to the Cyclops (who had only one eye each) and the Hecatonchires (the hundred-handed monsters, each of which sprouted fifty heads on its shoulders). This was excess, proliferation, monstrosity. Hence, Uranus "hated" his children from the very first day: "and every time each one was beginning to come out, he would push them back again, deep inside Gaia, and would not let them into the light" (*Theogony* 156–158).

Uranus rejected his children, pushed them away, back into the deep darkness of the Earth. Gaia, however, became weary of this "burden" that Uranus concealed in her depths, and she devised "an evil, treacherous attack': she brought forth from within herself a sharp sickle of gray flint and said to her children, "My sons . . . if you are willing to obey me, we can punish your father for the brutal treatment he put upon you, for he was first to think of shameful dealing" (*Theogony* 160, 164–166). The children were frightened and spoke never a word. Only Kronos, the "great devious-devising Kronos," was ready to do the deed. And "giant Gaia rejoiced greatly in her heart" (*Theogony* 173). She concealed him, placed him in an ambush, handed him the sickle, "and told him all her treachery" (*Theogony* 175).

And when "desiring love [Uranus] . . . embraced Gaia and lay over her stretched out complete," Kronos reached out with his left hand and seized him, and "holding in his right the enormous sickle with its long blade edged like teeth, he swung it sharply, and lopped the members of his own father" (*Theogony* 175–181).

Thus he brought about the separation of father and mother, Heaven and Earth. With this, he also ended the excessive fertility of the primordial time of origins. Kronos cast Uranus's genitals behind him into the sea. From them Aphrodite (Venus), the "foam-born," later arose. From the drops of blood that fell from the wound on Mother Earth new creatures arose: the Erinyes (goddesses of vengeance), the Melic Nymphs, and twenty-four giants. And thus the uncontainable creative force reappeared.

Kronos (Saturn)

A new age began with the castration of Uranus: Heaven and Earth were now separated. In the place of abundance, excess, and timelessness, Kronos now instituted measure and measured time. He established his dominion, made regulations, and set limits; he banished everything threatening and all competitors to Tartaros, the underworld. He held his brothers in chains and ruled as sole authority, as king.

Rhea, one of the daughters of Uranus and Gaia, wed him (Rhea, again, meant Earth). But Kronos lived in fear. He knew that he, too, would be castrated by a strong son and robbed of his power, for Uranus and Gaia had predicted so.

Kronos was now concerned with his own security, with self-preservation, with assuring his sphere of absolute influence. He did not think of the future. Anything new appeared suspect. He consumed the children that Rhea brought into the world, swallowing them as soon as they left her womb: Hestia, Demeter, Hera, Hades, and Poseidon.

But when Rhea again became pregnant and was about to give birth to her sixth child, Zeus, she turned to her parents, Uranus and Gaia, for advice. Gaia, the earth itself, took up her cause and advised Rhea to go to Lyktos on Crete the day of the birth and to bring the child into the world there. Immediately following the birth, Rhea hid Zeus in an inaccessible grotto that she had found there "in the depths of the holy Earth." Instead of bringing Kronos her child, Rhea swaddled a great stone and Kronos swallowed it without noticing the difference between rock and baby, so powerfully driven was he by his drive to power and so distant from everything living.

Zeus (Jupiter)

Zeus was nourished in that grotto on the milk of a goat and reared by nymphs and grew rapidly into a "mighty lord." Now, in his full strength, he went to his father and deposed him as had been prophesied. But he did not simply repeat his father's deed: he did not "unman" him, but rather disempowered him; he deposed him as ruler and king. But first, with the help of a ruse, he compelled Kronos to disgorge the children he had swallowed. Zeus served him a potion that made him vomit out everything, starting with the stone he had swallowed. Then Zeus also liberated his father's brothers from their fetters and as token of their gratitude received thunder and lightning from them, henceforth the tokens of his power.

Saturn and His Children
Woodcut by Hans Sebald Beham, ca. 1530

There are various accounts of the way Zeus subsequently dealt with his father. One account tells that Zeus banished him to the underworld where he remained forever.

Hesiod tells that, after a period of time, Kronos took up arms and challenged the previously fettered Titans to battle because he refused to grant Zeus rulership. The battle lasted ten years, and Zeus was about to be defeated and himself fettered when, at Gaia's bidding, the Hecatonchires, the children "hidden" from Uranus, were summoned from the underworld. They helped destroy the Titans.

The erupting chaos of the war is depicted impressively: the might of the Hecatonchires, who could hurl three hundred stones at once, the power of the Titans: "the infinite great sea moaned terribly and the earth crashed aloud, and the wide sky resounded as it was shaken, and tall Olympus rocked on its bases in the fan of the wind of the immortals" (*Theogony* 678–681). At the height of the battle, and with lightning and thunder and mighty roaring, Zeus was able to gain the victory, again quiet the Elements, and cause a new order to arise. Thereupon "by the advice of Gaia," Zeus was promoted "to be King and rule over the immortals," master of Olympus (*Theogony* 884). All acknowledged him as the supreme ruler.

In another version, Zeus made peace with Kronos from the very beginning. True, he did bind him, but he then sent him to the Islands of the Blessed at the ends of the earth. "There the breezes of Oceanus blew about the tower of Kronos. There he is king, the husband of Rhea" (Kerenyi 1951, p. 30).

In a later variant, Zeus sent his father to Latinum (the present-day Italy) and granted him that land as his own. Thus, he appeared to divide the realm with him: Kronos received a large area indeed, but it was mountainous and unfruitful.

Kronos then devoted all his energies and his stubborn survival ability to the task of making that land fruitful. He taught humankind agriculture, and he married Ops, the goddess of sowing and harvesting grain. From then on, he had so many tasks and projects and was so occupied with his work—he also received the devotion due him—that he no longer meddled in the Olympian "affairs" or "games." In Latinum he was coregent with Janus, who looked both forward and backward, the turning point in the course of time.

Following his victory over the chaos of war and the primordial powers of prehistory, the world was ordered anew. Zeus divided rulership between himself and his two brothers.

He himself remained lord of the skies; Poseidon (Neptune)

Jupiter and His Children
Woodcut by Hans Sebald Beham, ca. 1530

became god of the seas; Hades was the god of the underworld.
The earth belonged to all in common, as did Olympus, the mountain of the gods (*Iliad* 15.186–193).

16

Poseidon (Neptune)

Poseidon became lord of the seas and also lord of the springs and rivers, which ultimately empty into the sea or disappear into the earth. He was called "Embracer of the Earth" and "Sustainer of the Earth," for water surrounded the earth everywhere. His attribute was the trident. With it, he could churn up the seas and cause storms, cover the earth and sea with clouds, make the storm-lashed waves tower up, and even cause the earth to shudder. With his trident, he could also subdue everything, pacify it, immerse it in fog, and blanket it in forgetfulness.

Three paces, which made the mountains tremble, took Poseidon from Olympus to his home, his castle at the bottom of the sea. Joyfully the seas opened when he approached. The sea creatures and the monsters from the deep gathered and played before their master. Poseidon was unfathomable and easily agitated. He could be annoyed and ill-willed, and fisherfolk and mariners feared him. But he could also bring rescue to those in distress at sea.

Poseidon propagated his line with goddesses, nymphs, and human daughters. He deceived his first wife, Amphitre, who he had won at great effort, and engaged in new amorous adventures. With Medusa he procreated the steed Pegasus, so named because it was born near the waters, the pegai of Oceanus. Poseidon was called "Lord" or "Subduer of Horses." He harnessed his team, mounted his golden chariot, and drove over the waves, and the axle of his chariot never got wet. Poseidon roamed about, sometimes leaving the sea, and was now here, now there. He acknowledged Zeus as the Lord of Olympus, but—when necessary—put him in his place. Occasionally, he obliterated boundaries and made claims to a piece of land here or a city there. However he did submit to judgments and appeared to forget until something new excited him.

Hades (Pluto)

Hades, the oldest brother of Zeus, became the god of the underworld, the land of the dead, of all that lies beneath and in the earth. Here dwell the Hecatonchires, the hundred-handed monsters, "Zeus's trustworthy sentinels"; here the uncanny and vanquished things of prehistory lie buried. This is where the spectral dead live. Here no mortal may enter. Even the gods avoid the gloomy, uncanny place, the fathomless abyss beneath the sea, the earth, and the heavens. It is "a great chasm," and "once one were inside the gates of it within a whole year's completion he would not come to the bottom" (*Theogony* 740–742).

Here Night has her darksome house; here Sleep and Death, her children, are at home. But from here Morning of the day sets forth, "and the house never at once contains both of them, but at every time, while one of them is out of the house, faring over the length of the earth, the other remains indoors" (*Theogony* 751–753).

Hades set foot on the earth only once: when he seized Persephone and abducted her to his realm. He did not even let himself be seen on Olympus. He remained in his underworld, in Hades; he is one with it, unseen by mortals. To him belonged the cap or helmet of invisibility given him by the Titans (which later he gave or lent to Hermes).

But Hades, in a later manifestation (Pluto), was also the lord of the treasures concealed in the earth and of all those things that come out of the earth: master of the earth's power to grant blessings, hence of grain. As lord of all these potential riches, he had the horn of plenty as his emblem.

At the end of these earliest times, the universe had grown large; heaven, earth, and underworld had moved far apart: "Such is the distance from earth's surface to gloomy Tartaros. For a brazen anvil dropping out of the sky would take nine nights, and nine days, and land on earth on the tenth day, and a brazen anvil dropping off the earth would take nine nights, and nine days, and land in Tartaros on the tenth day" (*Theogony* 721–725).

These are the vast "spaces"—inner and outer—that were divided up under Zeus's rulership among the various powers, each according to his capacity and inclination, and in which psychic life could now run its course.

The Psychological View of Creation Myths

Uranus

Our myth of the beginnings in the images of Gaia and Uranus, like every archetype, cannot be simply translated into psychological language but, at first, only circumambulated imaginally.

The primordial given is Earth and Heaven, or matter and spirit, fixed and moving. In this we can also see our "earthly" reality, our concrete limitedness as well as a power that completely surpasses us. We are incapable of encountering this power consciously. It takes its nourishment "at night," in the dark, when we are unconscious. It becomes visible only in its "children," that is, a conscious *Auseinandersetzung* takes place only when we come into contact with the results, the "progeny," of this encounter.

Uranus can be realized only through his effects on the earth. Our bodily existence is the prerequisite for an archetypal structure—something that informs us—to be able to take shape in us as an image, to be able to propagate itself in us as movement or as something moving in us.

Not everyone becomes conscious of these inner workings: at first, children remain hidden in the caves of the earth. And if one looks into the caves, one may be alarmed. It is not everyone's cup of tea to confront and come to terms with unpleasant thoughts or uncanny notions—with the "hundred-handed" or the "fifty-headed" or the "one-eyed" monsters.

Saturn is needed then to create boundaries, structure, and overview. First the conscious "I," the ego, must be delimited: staking out one's own territory, setting one's boundaries as a person. As one does this, everything that is too threatening is "fettered" or banished into the underworld, into the unconscious—and only in a later stage of consciousness, with Jupiter, can it again be let in and eventually even employed usefully. Uranus as a psychic function can be experienced as inspiration or as creative power, but also as a feeling of being overwhelmed by too many ideas and impulses, as rampant creativity.

Under Uranus's reign, the "hundred-handed" creatures— that is, excessive impetus—come into being. These beings have fifty heads each: a frightening abundance of ideas. Uranus himself conceals these children in the earth; thus germinal possibilities are contained in us that can surprise us by erupting at any time as uncontrolled emotions, as revolting ideas, as breakthroughs to new developments. Discoveries and inventions can arise that reveal so much explosive Uranian power one must return them to subterranean storerooms. "The deep caverns of Earth" must then conceal such dangerous things.

Things that can save may also be "buried" in us: potentials and strengths, which motivate us in hundreds of ways to be steadfast in the battle between chaos and meaningful survival. Thus it is that the "hundred-handed" creatures came in response to the Earth's advice just in time to help Jupiter achieve his victory when he was about to be defeated in his battle with Saturn and the Titans.

The astrological interpretation of Uranus focuses on the surprising, the unexpected, and the chance event. Uranus works his effects outside of causality and continuity.

To Uranus belongs the element of incalculability: he comes when he pleases—and stays away when he pleases. Most certainly one cannot deliberately summon or coerce his influence (not even when a good idea is ever so sorely needed). Likewise, one cannot hinder unsettling thoughts or deeds by instituting security measures.

Uranian power can break forth from the unknown, unconscious background in the form of thoughts or deeds, for weal or woe, without limitation or control. (Uranian power is often perceived only later via other psychological functions.)

Under Uranus's influence the issue is not permanence but ever and again the new, radical change, departure, the future—even if it may terrify.

This can be related to any area of life (depending on Uranus's location in the horoscope). Uranus can release sudden impulses or effect sudden self-revelations, or bring about inspiration as well as irritation via a Thou or other persons. Uranus can reveal himself in playful possibilities, creative impulses, and in sudden ideas urgent to be thought through. These ideas can mean change and revolution, in the personal as well as in the social sphere. They can relate to the world around us or to inner attitudes.

Where, how intensely, and how clearly one experiences something stemming from the Uranian principle depends on Uranus's position in the horoscope, on its constellation with other psychic functions, and on the level on which the person concerned experiences it and is able to work it through. Fifty-headed ideas and hundred-handed motivations can be so frightening for many people that they cannot make them conscious, or must again quickly repress them into the depths of the soul. Other persons discover the extraordinary range of human possibilities in just such experiences.

Saturn

Individual history begins only with the appearance of Saturn. What is necessary is the "tower of strength" who can separate himself from the primordial unity of mother and father; he "sees" and hence can put an end to the unity. (Gaia had alerted him: she had summoned.)

The wish for eternal oneness is linked with the origin of existence: the oneness of the "children" with the mother, taken back into the deep caverns of the Earth.

This original unity becomes unstable when Gaia feels "burdened" and no longer wants to bear the burden. At that point, she turns against what has complemented her and enveloped her, against the masculine principle, against Uranus. The urge toward further development arises out of oppression. The Earth must oppose Heaven, the feminine principle against the masculine.

But although Gaia creates the sharp sickle that will bring about the separation from within of herself, she does not harvest the fruits of her labors. That would be the end, a negation of what had been heretofore. What is needed is a further development, specifically of the masculine principle. What is necessary is differentiation in the son, in the next generation, and this means a new level of development. If this succeeds, then greater possibilities are available to the Earth, too: concrete, conscious life, individuality, development, history.

Strength is necessary to perform this sort of incisive act: the power of a great individual, of a strong "I." And emotion is necessary, too, for motivation. Saturn "hates" his father. He does not slay Uranus in all aspects, but he "kills" the father role in him. He emasculates him. Now no longer Uranus but only Saturn can procreate—or so it seems. Saturn is now king.

Freud (1938) called the murder of the father the "primary and primordial crime of humanity as of the individual," the source of guilt feelings and again and again of new anxiety. Patricide has always existed and must always exist, for life that is manifesting and becoming real leads to concrete *Auseinandersetzung*, to confrontation and conflict and having it out. It leads to the experience of guilt and suffering.

Addressing the "heavenly powers," Goethe writes:

> *You guide us into life,*
> *And make the innocent guilty,*
> *Then hand us over to our pain:*
> *For on Earth all guilt is avenged.*
> *(Goethe 1950, p. 345)*

In order to come into his own life, Saturn must oppose the father so single-mindedly that he can live only in opposition to him and must prevail against the creative principle. All the strong masculine characteristics that he develops are directed against the primordial paternal principle.

As an individual who has become guilty, Saturn is no longer contained and embraced in the tribe, in the clan, in the community. He must keep all others at a distance; he must tether, banish, and confine the titanic forces of his "siblings." It is a difficult task for Saturn to maintain himself as a lone individual, to prevail against all the others, to protect and secure himself. He must concentrate all his powers on the mastery of this situation. He becomes isolated.

Fear makes him narrow and restrictive. He can count only on himself; he must devour what could be his future: his children. This means he prevents further life. Like so many tyrants, Saturn is powerless in his power.

By order of Mother Earth, whose own self-preservation was at stake, Saturn undertook too much (although it became a question of his survival). She had given him a harvesting tool and had shown him the cunning ploy by means of which he was to help her. Following the execution of that ploy, the earthly cycle was supposed to continue for ever: Saturn in place of his father, Jupiter in place of Saturn, and so on—and the Gaias and the Rheas would always know what to do to find completion and rejuvenation in their children. For them, it would be a question of cyclical return and of individual development. The son always replaces the spouse, but not to become an autonomous and independent man or husband.

Saturn took his task seriously and accomplished the incisive division of the original unity. But after this castration, fear overtook him. He threw the severed member "behind him" into the sea. He cast it from his sight, he submerged it in the depths, he "repressed" his deed. The act of casting it behind him seems like a defense mechanism, or an apotropaic magical act against the Erinyes who will yet arise out of his father's blood and oppose him. By casting the genitals behind him, Saturn believes he can leave them behind, get rid of them, and does not even imagine what he has thrown away, what living beauty, what passions of love and procreative joy could have arisen from them. Unfortunately, that remains hidden from Saturn's sight.

Instead, Saturn compulsively watches over his power. He "thinks" in causal-mechanical terms: an eye for an eye, a tooth for a tooth. The swallows up everything spontaneous, everything that is awakening to life, and he develops specific behaviors and compulsions. He has a rigid image of the enemy; he rearms; he is constantly on guard.

So, too, in the course of history, as humankind misunderstands its domination of Mother Earth, and we get tyrannical power, sterile patriarchy, narrowness and one-sidedness. The same thing can happen in one form or another to any individual at various periods in life.

Whenever there seems to be no future, Mother Earth always knows what to do: Zeus is born, a new possibility that turns things around. For this to happen, some preconditions must exist: Gaia and Rhea, the mothers, who want to preserve life, provide protection during the first days of life—in the deep cave—and friendly dealings with the feminine—be it nymphs or nurturing goats. Thus it is that divine spontaneity and self-assurance of instinct develop in Zeus.

Accordingly, Jupiter can depose a petrified, rigid, old regime with natural strength, lightning, thunder, and lots of roaring, and with clever tricks without renouncing the values he holds: he once more dispenses with whatever good possibilities had accumulated in the patriarchy.

Saturn's further history, the role that will fall to his lot, remains open. Again, viewed astrologically, how Saturn reveals himself to the individual depends upon the relationships among the "gods" and on the level at which the individual concerned follows and understands the "discourse of the gods."

If it happens that Saturn is simply relieved of his sovereignty and deposed, he remains a "grumbling old man" in the underworld; from the unconscious he will cause his displeasure to be felt. If Saturn is jovially dispatched to the land of the blessed, he may have a pleasant sojourn, but his life experiences and powers remain unused, and they atrophy. The opportunity for consciousness, for working through life problems, is lost. Marital harmony, "honeymoon on the beach," is a return to the beginning, a regression to the primordial unity.

If Saturn has us in his power and is mistrustful toward us and toward the world around us, or excessively ambitious and presumptuous, life turns into a battlefield. Hundredfold powers are misused, the "elements" get in a uproar. It signifies an elemental threat when a destructive power in us becomes power-hungry, when we are cornered and become rigid, when we get caught in complexes.

Whenever one sole function predominates in the interplay of functions, the others become inferior, and equilibrium and possible wholeness are menacingly upset.

We need a lot of Jupiter's intelligence to address unloved, unadapted traits in ourselves, to confront our shadow, to put troublesome functions to work. When they are given a "territory," a place in which they are utilized, Saturn can work his effects an entire lifetime and ultimately perhaps yield a profit: rich harvest. But it may also take a lifetime to experience this.

It would be wrong to construe Saturn as an "image of the enemy," to see in him the "evil" principle, as earlier astrologers have done. Saturn is necessary for any individual development whatsoever to take place. We need him so that we can consciously set limits and boundaries vis-à-vis the overwhelming abundance of what surrounds us, the current that would pull us back into the collective. Saturn is necessary because through him we are ever and again forced concretely to come to terms with the shadow in us—to come to consciousness.

Everybody has a saturnine component. Even if we want to cast it behind us, it still gazes at us from our natal chart. This is fortunate, for we can observe its various aspects and gain from it whatever of its contents are valuable.

Jupiter's various confrontations with Saturn reveal that this is no easy undertaking. A successful integration of saturnine sides of our personality depends on the attitude with which we approach Saturn, and above all on how strongly and vitally Jupiter can develop in us.

The more alive the myth is for us, the more acutely we will perceive saturnine tendencies as psychic structures and incorporate them in our astrological interpretation.

In undertaking this, it has proven useful at first to ignore the content and to visualize the *tendencies to movement* inherent in the saturnine "essence." But even this must always sound like a personification, since we are only able to "translate" one archetypal image into another sort of imaginal language. Conceived of most generally, the movement underlying the saturnine principle is one proceeding from the outside inward. Saturn takes things into himself and incorporates them: he devours, swallows, digests, and processes. He concentrates, delimits, and isolates. He curtails, fetters, and captivates. He hinders, suppresses, and oppresses.

Saturn contracts and compresses or condenses. The greater the density of a substance, the heavier it becomes (all this applies in the concrete as in the extended sense: materially and psychically). Lead—an especially heavy metal—was assigned to Saturn.

Employed positively, Saturn concentrates, disciplines, structures, erects, teaches, instructs, accumulates; he is tenacious, persevering; he prevails; but he is also unpretentious and unassuming. One could continue this list endlessly, but the symbolic image in the background makes excessive detail superfluous.

Saturn's limit-setting aspect was expressed allegorically in old depictions of the planets by showing him with the hourglass and the scythe, as a skeleton, Death.

But he also appears as a gardener with a sickle in his hand: he cuts the grass, provides for the future—but he also cuts back too much of a good thing, the weeds.

Saturn
Calendar illustration,
1514

The Saturnine quality is graphically presented, for example, in the green of conifers: the greatest possible volume of chlorophyll is collected in the smallest space, concentrated. This is not luxuriant abundance, but it endures, it is evergreen and outlasts the change of seasons.

Jupiter

Any movement always calls forth a countermovement. Saturn began under pressure: under the pressure of the mother who rebelled against her husband and incited her son against his father. Saturn dared to step from safety and protection into guilt. And he bore the consequences: fear, loneliness, denial of the future. Jupiter, on the other hand, was born "under a different star." From the outset, he was supported by the love of his mother, who wanted him. He was able to develop into a strong man because he was cared for and surrounded by positive feminine qualities, which he could let live in himself. He was not fixated on the "purely" masculine as was his patriarchal father because he did not have to make his way into life against it. His own power and strength grew; he did not need his mother's "sharp-toothed sickle."

Jupiter's attitude to life in its richness is affirming. He is not restricted to specific "useful" aspects; he knows no fear. He sets the Titans free without first reassuring himself that they will not kill him. And in return he receives thunder and lightning, their power, as a gift. When he needs them, he fetches out of the depths the uncanny powers that are ready to help him with their "hundred-handedness" because he accepted them. What for others signified danger are for him "reliable sentinels." In his new order, these sentinels voluntarily return to the depths, to their "dwelling," because here they are "at home."

With Jupiter, we come to a battle between old and new worlds, a battle between two fundamentally different human attitudes to life. Jupiter's victory brings a new order to the world, in which one-sidedness no longer rules, but rather multiplicity is possible. Here there is organic growth and organic order: from above and below, from heaven and earth, from the sea and the deep. His is a holistic world. He the "god of the immortals," which means the eternal life principle.

The myths from Uranus to Jupiter also reveal the path of the individual: from the primordial state of being contained and protected to the autonomous, self-reliant ego; into the world of good and evil, accomplishment and punishment, discipline and resistance, teaching and learning; until (in puberty) natural powers grow and the human individual now instinctively presses onward toward his or her own independent path in life—and achieves it, even against the resistance of the old "ruler." If a person develops freely, as did Jupiter, it is possible up to this point to appropriate from the old values whatever is useful—but thereafter the individual would preserve them in his or her own sense and develop them in a personal way. The individual would come to a differentiation of values.

If we attempt an astrological interpretation in terms of general *tendencies of movement*, the Jupiter principle reveals a movement leading outward from within: an opening and giving, permitting and blossoming. To Jupiter belongs organic growth and multiplicity, living order, building and development, actualization and discovery of meaning; fearlessness and openness toward the unfamiliar or foreign, or even strange and repellent.

If the evergreen suited Saturn, then the green of deciduous trees with their living changeability befits Jupiter. In the spring, they reveal themselves in all their richness with the freshest, brightest green; in autumn, they glow in bright colors; and in winter, when the tree is bare, the buds already contain the full vitality of the abundance of the next year.

Change and meaning are the essence of the Jupiter principle. Jupiter distributed the domains of the world in a meaningful way when Neptune and Pluto became the gods of the sea and the underworld.

The planets and gods temporally and spatially the farthest away are also those most distant in the soul. In them, we encounter the myths in ourselves that we actually only suspect, or retrospectively intuit, and are able to conceptualize but poorly. Many things may touch on early, scarcely knowable childhood memories, other things on dreams or archaic terrors. There are seams between consciousness and the unconscious, between the personal unconscious and the collective or cosmic unconscious, but they close up if willfully approached.

Uranus is the first planet no longer visible to the naked eye—and is humankind's first altogether overwhelming experience. From childhood on, we can be seized by Uranian emotion: sudden ideas "from above"—inspirations, religious emotions, illuminations—strike us and fall away from consciousness.

But then we really need saturnine confrontation and life experience, and Jupiter's consciousness and experience of oneself, to become aware that we are also determined by forces from the inner depths, from the unconscious.

Neptune and Pluto are the planets farthest from Earth. In the myth, they are Jupiter's brothers, but born before him. Through him, they come into relationship to Earth and to us. They are the powers that carry and support us from below—or unnerve and devour us. Neptune, as god of the sea, surrounds and holds the Earth; Pluto is the abyss, the one who ultimately carries everything back to himself. Corresponding to the various domains of activity, they represent various levels in the unconscious, if we may speak of them in such a localized manner.

In the new order of the world, Uranus is not mentioned very often. The gods from whom heaven was taken arise again from out of the deep. Ever since rationalization and mechanization of the world gained the upper hand, and heaven was stripped of its gods, fear and dread no longer come "from above" but out of the depths, for example, from the power of the masses that more and more threaten the life of the individual since the last century (approximately since the planet Neptune was discovered), or from the most intimate reaches of matter itself, from the atomic nucleus and from the possibility of splitting it (which was discovered about the same time the planet Pluto was). But there have been countercurrents: since the end of the last century, depth psychology has led to insights into the depths of the individual soul. And in response to the threat posed by the splitting of the atom, there has arisen in humankind an ever-increasing need for holistic experience that also always embraces polarities. The collective unconscious is the pole opposite collective consciousness; following rationalization and demythologization, the pendulum swings back toward myth, mysticism, and the esoteric. As is becoming increasingly evident, gradually penetrating collective consciousness, our confrontation and coming to terms with our own depths, with our unconscious, will be of decisive significance in deciding whether our world will be carried by the depths, or destroyed by them. At the outset, I attempted to show that coming to terms with psychic forces must not occur at the expense of our relationship to reality; rather, it becomes possible precisely when we take reality seriously and explore its secrets.

Neptune and Pluto are symbols for these depths and represent them in their various aspects.

Neptune

Neptune is the god of the broad seas, of rivers and springs. Under his dominion, the waters are animated and agitated. These waters of the deep now contain the creative power that previously was "in heaven": Uranus member fell into them. Venus grew up here, nourished by the foam, and set foot on land. Ever new contents and new creations arise: with every dream and every fantasy, in intimations and in images.

Neptune's waters extend from the clear, bright bubbling springs and rivers and streams to the sea that can be smooth and "friendly" but also agitated and roaring, the sea that no human can penetrate, that remains closed to human consciousness. Here, in the deepest depths, Neptune's castle is situated, his residence, the center from which he ascends and works his effects over and over again—now closer, now farther from humankind, closer to or farther from consciousness.

Neptune is incalculable. Sometimes he gives a rich catch and saves mariners in distress; sometimes he can draw them into the depths to their destruction. Helpful dreams can arise out of Neptune's waters, but also threatening moods which can devour a human. The waters can support or swallow, and we can be held or unnerved. Neptune was called "earth-sustainer" and "earth-shaker."

Psychologically translated as well as astrologically understood, Neptune is still contained in these images, and his workings can still be recognized in the varied forms of water.

As lord of the moving waters, Neptune is lord of movement and oscillation. In him, we experience anything that reaches us in waves: whatever we perceive with our senses (sound, color, smell, stimuli of all sorts) or whatever we intuitively grasp (moods in ourselves, the emotional atmosphere around us, oscillations in space and in people).

Neptune can awaken our intuition, sharpen our subliminal perceptions, open us to experiences that lie outside of causality and space–time conditionality. But becoming one with the sea and the waves can also signify immersion in fantasy and daydreams, a regressive submersion. Neptune can inundate, enshroud in fog, and plunge into twilight. He entices us to conceal and to mask things. Likewise, he can pull us back into the collective and seduce us into collective emotionality.

Neptune's waters also dissolve: they loosen and give wing, or they lead to dissolution when the ego's boundaries are abolished and contours blend. A loss of boundaries or boundlessness is lived as a mystical experience, as intoxication and ecstasy, but also as deception and madness, and above all as passion in every form.

Thus, Neptune as a symbol can be experienced in greatly differing ways: as the highest prize or the greatest loss, depending on how the gods converse with Neptune, and on what plane or at which time the soul of the individual responds.

Pluto

Pluto, the god of the underworld, was first called Hades. In Greek, Hades means "invisible" as well as "to make invisible." Hades himself is invisible, either by the power of his cloak of invisibility or because he does not show himself to men and gods. Similarly, his place, also called Hades, is invisible: no mortal can enter there and depart alive. The contents of Hades remain invisible to us: here dwell the shades and the dead; we hear of them or have premonitions, but we cannot see them. Thus, a boundary intervenes between Hades and our conscious experience.

29

The darkness of night arises out of Hades, and here the light of day vanishes. Earth and sea have their roots here in the darkness; but Hades's darkness is deeper yet than the deepest of seas, the deepest abyss, inaccessible, incomprehensible. What is dark and invisible causes *Angst.* Even the immortals feared and avoided Hades and his dismal place. One dares venture only as far as the portals of his underworld, and even that only for a cogent reason.

The totally unknown, totally invisible is also the totally unconscious. Here, in the deepest depths, the threatening heritage of primeval times, of the ancestors, is "en-graved," here the patterns of human experience are preformed. Here, in the realm of the collective unconscious, the archetypes are "rooted" (if we may speak so graphically of abstract structures). In the unconscious, the primordial potential of human experience, an ancient river of unsuspected motivations and forces, is "engrammed." These depths lie even lower than Neptune's domains.

In the myth, the underworld "carries" the earth as the earth carries the heavens; likewise, our psychic life is carried and destined by the underworld of the unconscious. Out of it the experiences of our soul and the images and thoughts rising into consciousness take their shape, as do those experiences that ultimately transcend consciousness.

When Hades was no longer experienced only as dreadful and horrid, when people were able to connect with him more consciously and to recognize the abundance and the riches under the earth, he was called Pluto. The horn of plenty became his insignia. This aspect reveals the milder side of the chthonic powers.

Both poles belong to the workings of Plutonian power. Pluto can draw one into darkness or let abundance ascend into the light. In him, a person can be swallowed or held captive by the unconscious, or ever new things can emerge into consciousness. The two poles can be held in the image of night and breaking day or in the image of the metamorphosis of a seed that first must perish in the dark earth in order to grow into a new form in the light.

Likewise, astrologically, "transformation of shape" in the widest sense of the phrase is associated with Pluto, whether the form is destroyed or brought forth anew. Both Pluto's destructive, threatening, fear-inspiring side and—as a possibility—his beneficent sides must be seen.

The two extreme poles of Pluto's workings are revealed in the tendency to descend, extinguish, destroy (also to darken and to make invisible) and in the ascending explosive and germinating power, increase in energy, and the capacity to break through and prevail.

In Pluto, we find the end or the abundance of life.

Jupiter (Zeus): New World Order

At the end of the primordial period, the universe, and the interior space of the soul, had become great.

With Jupiter, a new order of the world appears, a new division of the various domains among the various powers, a new outline of the individual and of the cosmic interplay of all. Heaven, sea, and underworld have separated, and upon the earthly stage many forms of life can now develop. The gods have moved closer to humankind, their domains can be experienced; but with this development, the human individual and human fate move closer to the gods. The human being becomes a central concern of the myths and legends, such as those Homer recounts, for example.

What was originally experienced in the history of both the race and the individual as something mysterious, lying "outside" as a numinous phenomenon appearing in the gods or the planets, has now moved not only into humankind's vicinity but is alive in human beings. Already in Homer's epics, the inner and outer spaces often intermingle: a god assumes human form; divine energies work their effects in humans. Often it is scarcely possible to distinguish the divine from the human: only a glance, only a particular gesture allows the observer to tell the difference.

Under Jupiter's rulership the possibilities for experience begin to unfold. Now there are many places and players. And all "places" and testimonies of his workings taken together constitute a unity: a cosmos, outside and within the human person. Jupiter—as we have already seen—let repressed life return to life and made development possible where previously there was restriction, imprisonment, and darkness. Under Jupiter's rulership there is neither rigid limit nor chaotic, overflowing excess. Each of the Olympian deities receives his or her own domain and can bring his or her specific qualities into the interplay of all. Each divine power has its own function and reflects one possibility of human experiencing. Jupiter himself sees to it that each receives his or her due and that even unwritten laws are observed, that order and meaning are maintained.

Form-giving primal images, archetypes, are also constellated in the "younger" gods who were associated with the planets closer to Earth: Mars, Venus, and Mercury, the descendants of Jupiter and his generation. It is in them that the divine manifests in ever more human domains, in proximity to humankind; that is, they are closer to consciousness. When, for example, we think of the functions of Mars, Venus, and Mercury in us, we are dealing with ever more "personal" domains. In our daily life, we so often take them for granted that it is hard to recognize the "divine primordial image" in them. They are all facets of Jupiter: he sired them, made them possible, let them in. "By the advice of Gaia . . . he distributed among [the Immortals] their titles and privilege" (*Theogony* 883–885).

Jupiter as the Origin and Possibility of Developing Various Aspects of Life

Not only did things in general develop under Jupiter's dominion, he himself "developed" and produced progeny with goddesses, demi-goddesses, and humans. From the various unions arose just as many new possibilities.

Jupiter's first lover was Metis, wisdom. It was she who gave him the draught that caused Saturn to vomit up the children he had swallowed. But when she was pregnant, the old fear that had plagued Saturn now overtook Jupiter: Uranus and Gaia had predicted for him, too, that he would fear the birth of "a son to be King over gods and mortals . . . and his heart would be overmastering" (*Theogony* 897–898). As contemporary psychology might put it, the "family inheritance," the "early childhood trauma" that even a god has difficulty overcoming, is revealed here. It seems Jupiter has to carry on the conflict of the generations; it is so difficult to make room for new developments and to break patterns of behavior. Nevertheless, Jupiter, for his part, does not simply repeat what his father did: he does not devour the newborn child; rather, even before its birth, he swallows the goddess herself along with the child in her. And what he thus incorporates is Metis, wisdom. For future conflicts, this could signify greater magnanimity and presence of mind, greater wisdom. "Zeus put her away inside his own belly so that this goddess should think for him, for good and for evil" (*Theogony* 899–900).

But first, Jupiter himself had to carry the fruit of his liaison to term and birth it: when the time had come, his head seemed to burst with pain, and he cried out aloud. Poseidon/Neptune of the depths of the sea had to cleave his head so that Athena could be born from it. Hence, Jupiter's first child was, in the truest sense of the word, a brainchild, whose birth was possible only through the midwifery of the sea god, with help from the depths. But after Jupiter had endured the birth itself and the pains it entailed, his anxiety about further new creations and progeny was obviously overcome. With Themis, goddess of justice, he procreated the fates and the goddesses of growth; with Eurynome, the graces; with Mnemosyne, the Muses; with Demeter, Persephone; with Leto, Apollo and Artemis; and later, in many different forms, yet other divine or heroic possibilities.[7]

But first, Zeus wedded Hera, a daughter of Kronos (Saturn). This marriage was enduring, but often unhappy. Hera watched over her husband jealously and attempted to direct his attention solely toward herself, at which, to her sorrow, she was not always successful. Then she followed him with anger and passion, and shamed him unscrupulously. As befitted her paternal heritage, she tried to exclude, dispel, and annihilate everything unbefitting. For example, she magically changed beautiful Io, who was pleasing to Jupiter, into a cow in order to remove her from Jupiter's sight. By trickery she caused the death of Semele, who was pregnant by Zeus; but Zeus took the unborn child into himself, carrying it in his thigh until term, and gave birth to Dionysus. The old tension between Saturn and Jupiter, between the narrow patriarchal spirit and the open-hearted matriarchal spirit, lives on in Zeus and Hera in this marriage, but it was always endured and reconciled again and again.

One fruit of this relationship, this union of opposites, that turned out well was the daughter Hebe, "eternal youth," whom

Hercules later married. She was a faithful wife, a good mother, and the couple spent their old age happily together.

It is otherwise with Jupiter's and Hera's son Mars, unbeloved of the gods and men, the "shield smasher," the god of battle. But he, too, experienced justice at the hands of his father, as did the other Olympians.

When Jupiter arbitrates, each gets his due, for Jupiter judges according to the living situation and not by rigid laws. He allows the opposites to coexist, for movement, life, and growth is possible only in a dynamic situation. Jupiter grants the most divergent possibilities room to unfold, "prerogative and honor," for he rules with the wisdom that he has incorporated and that advises him "for weal or woe." Only bright and dark, light and shadow result in an organic whole.

*Jupiter
Book of Planets,
1553.*

Viewed psychologically and understood astrologically, the function of Jupiter in us makes possible a new orientation: escape from dead ends, from narrowness and from being stuck, from stagnation and rigidity. With Jupiter, there arises the question of meaning and the interdependency of meaning, of living possibilities of life, of development and of completeness—and that implies making room for vexatious aspects; indeed, even for ominous possibilities as long as they contain a point of departure from which they can turn toward the positive.

The Jupiter principle implies, above all, the unprejudiced openness to polar opposites such as male and female, good and evil ("weal and woe"). As we have seen, Jupiter offers himself as an example: as "lord" of heaven, of Olympus, and of thunder and lightning (which belong to the male principle), he is from the beginning nourished and strengthened by female qualities and later integrates as his first female quality, Metis, his "female wisdom." Fear that the male principle would gain the upper hand had driven him to it, fear of the son "overflowing with strength" who was expected, although Metis had expected a daughter, Athena, whom Zeus later bore from his head, a daughter with outstanding male qualities.

Thanks to the potion brewed by Wisdom which made Saturn release the children he had swallowed, the old values are at

Jupiter's disposal anew, but they must be accepted as his responsibility. New orientation means overcoming old, entrenched patterns of behavior and rigid norms; breakthrough to broad-mindedness; admission of polar possibilities so that wholeness becomes possible.

By incorporating Metis, Jupiter had indeed internalized the feminine—under the double aspect of the maternal and the tender future daughter—but this first step toward becoming whole was not entirely without its difficulties. Problematic not only was the birth from his head, but also the nature of the daughter herself, whom Hesiod calls "Athena of the gray eyes," "great goddess, weariless" who takes pleasure in the carnage and the battle (*Theogony* 924). She had turned out not much different from a strong-hearted son, differing only in that she acknowledged Zeus as father, shared the power, and did not compete with him.

The subsequent births bring a diverse unfolding of female qualities: the Graces are charm, attractiveness, and cheerfulness; the Hours embody the changes of growth over time; the Fates grant the individual his or her portion of good and evil and impose upon one the responsibility for carrying one's own destiny; with Kore, whom Jupiter "of wise counsel" let Hades abduct, he pays his due—or tribute—to the underworld. Through Jupiter, the feminine is born into all areas of life. Artemis, "the huntress," belongs in this group just as do the Muses, the goddesses "whose pleasure is all delightfulness, and the sweetness of singing" (*Theogony* 917).

Accordingly, Jupiter can also engage in very concrete *Auseinandersetzung* with the feminine part in himself that still carries a saturnine heritage, with his other, if perhaps not better, half, Hera. This signifies bonding, not only nonbinding pleasure; in Hebe, the daughter, eternal youth, it means eternal renewal, eternal beginning. It also means *Auseinandersetzung* and conflict, not only harmony and peace; thus, Mars (Ares), the god of war, is her son. Marriage with Hera demands the acceptance of even the foreign, uncomfortable, opposing forces—and a creative intercourse with them; and again and again the renewed reconciliation of the opposites.

Jupiter's two sons—Apollo and Dionysus—show that opposites can be joined together in the course of life, that becoming whole or complete is possible under Jupiter's aegis. Apollo, the firstborn son by Leto, and Dionysus, gestated and birthed by Zeus, reveal the proximity of the Apollonian and Dionysian natures in Zeus himself, the closeness of reflection and intoxication, of clear repose and possession. The proximity of these two opposites which limit each other found its expression in Delphi, where Dionysus was taken into the sacred precinct beside Apollo.

We can get some indication of the form and the area of life where the individual's development to the greatest possible wholeness lies by observing the position of Jupiter in the natal chart. Under the "star of Jupiter," work on a burdensome heritage, *Auseinandersetzung* with old conflicts, or inner tensions can lead to a fruitful process in which tethered powers can be set free and opposites can enter a fertile exchange. Conflict, strife, and disappointment form part of the process of *Auseinandersetzung*, but again and again they also give rise to new impulses. Granted, this is also true: *Quod licet Jovi non licet bovi* (What is permitted Jupiter is not permitted the ox). But it is not every person's lot to have Jupiter's function signify this sort of creative drive, nor does wholeness necessarily carry a divine aura.

Ares (Mars)

Ares is the only son of Zeus and Hera. He was, from the very beginning, an unloved child. Hera did not like him because he was rowdy, unruly, boisterous, and disobedient. Nobody was a match for his unpredictable pugnacity.

Many sources tell of a twin sister of Mars, Eris (conflict), who like her brother loved conflict for its own sake. She sought conflict and spread rumors in order to facilitate new engagements for Mars.

Mars was unbeloved not only of the gods but also of men. There were few shrines where he was worshiped. (They arose in great numbers only later in Rome where, after Jupiter, he was the most powerful god.) The Greeks placed him in Thrace, in the land of the barbarians who loved war for its own sake.

Poets have preferred to ignore Ares/Mars. Only when they speak of the army does Ares appear; he is present in the army; he is the army—an impersonal, destructive force. Whenever he is wounded, Mars bellows "like ten thousand men." Mars in not a god of war in the sense that he incites his people to battle and victory or, as a moral force, strengthens the warlike spirit. He is representative of the passion for conflict as such. Mars does not take sides. He is called "fickle" because he fights first with the

Mars and His Children
Woodcut by Hans Sebald Beham, ca. 1530

Greeks, then with the Trojans, impartially. It is said of him that he takes pleasure in murder and manslaughter. Once, when he lamented to Jupiter that he had been unjustly treated, Jupiter turned him away: "Don't burden me with your whining, Fickle

One, most hateful of all the gods who inhabit Olympus. For you take pleasure only in war and conflict . . . . Were you the son of another god and not my own son, you would long since be lying deeper than Uranus's sons lie" (Moritz, p. 96).

And yet, Mars belongs among the twelve Olympian gods, and Jupiter, who sired him, takes his stand in affirming that the destructive element also exists. Under Jupiter, there are the light and the dark forces in Olympus, within himself, and equally in his daughter, Athena, who was often called "prudent wisdom" but who also did not avoid the battlefield, or even the slaughter itself. When enraged Mars once attacked her shield with a lance, "she lifted up a huge boundary-stone in her hand, heaved it at the war god's forehead so that he collapsed and covered seven yolk of land" (Moritz, p. 93).

Mars is definitely vulnerable and can be vanquished by humans, mortals. The Aloadae bound him and held him prisoner for thirteen months. He would have starved and perished in humiliation if Mercury had not freed him. Diomedes wounded him in the Trojan War. And so Mars must ever and again flee to Olympus to save himself. Only Hades takes pleasure in the doings of the war god; after all, so many dead enter his realm thanks to Mars. But whenever Mars suffers a real injustice—as at the hands of Cadmus, king of Thebes—he can count on Jupiter's fair judgment.

When Cadmus slays a dragon sacred to Mars, Jupiter orders that Cadmus serve Mars for one year (some say four or eight years) as a slave. This means Cadmus must become intimately familiar with that power whose representative he simply wanted to conquer. Although Athena was able to extinguish Mars's blood-thirstiness a bit and set limits to his bellicosity, here she attends to a new dynamic. On her advice, Cadmus sows the dragon's teeth in a field, and from them sprout a hundred armed warriors. But these kill each other off in blind rage until only five remain, who later become the ancestral heroes of Thebes. After completing his service to Mars, King Cadmus finally gets Mars's most beautiful daughter as a wife: Harmonia, the daughter of Aphrodite, of Mars and Venus.

This seemingly one-sided destructive force has another side. In Ares (Mars) the unloved, in the rejected brawler, there awakens a longing for completion and liberation, for pleasure and love. He desires Aphrodite (Venus) who calms storms and can create peace and harmony. She is his counterpart and opposite pole, his complement in everything.

Ares (Mars) courts with desire and initiative—and with

39

success, although Aphrodite (Venus) had long been married to Hephaestus, the smith god, also a son of Hera (Homer *Odyssey* 8.266–366).[8] He is a patient, or rather, less passionate spouse despite his love for Aphrodite, and the marriage remains childless; it is unfruitful.

In Ares and Hephaestus, Aphrodite's lover and husband, we encounter two of Saturn's grandsons: destructive rage and limping melancholy, violent covetousness and intolerance. For a long time, Hephaestus notices nothing of the love relationship between Ares and Aphrodite until Helios, the sun, discovers the couple in Ares's palace and brings their relationship to light, until the sun "throws light on it." Then Hephaestus contrives a ruse. He says he is going away, and when Ares and Aphrodite are united together in love, he secretly throws over them an artfully worked net of bronze, fine as a spider web but unbreakable. Thus the two are caught and unable to flee. Hephaestus, the cuckolded husband, calls the Olympians together to subject the lovers to the ridicule of the gods. He wants to humiliate them but also get his revenge: he demands Zeus return his marriage gifts. The Olympians are amused. Apollo teases Hermes/Mercury, who would gladly have changed places with Ares. Poseidon/Neptune falls violently in love with Aphrodite and vouches for Ares (in the hope he will be his heir). Zeus/Jupiter declares Hephaestus a fool for exposing his private affairs so publicly. Together they all depart the scene where, this time, intolerance had not been victorious. (The goddesses—indignant, discreet, embarrassed—had not even made an appearance.) But the relationship between Ares and Aphrodite, Mars and Venus, was not to be ended so lightly, for they were "as though made for each other" and, like polar opposites, continued to be attracted to each other.

Mars and Venus begat fear and terror: Deimos and Phobos. But Eros is also born, the boy who awakens love, whose magic no one can resist. His arrow is dipped in honey and gall: he brought sweetness and suffering to those he struck. In Eros we see, in yet another form, how every movement elicits its counter-movement. Eros remains a child until Venus, again from a union with Mars, bears Anteros, love reciprocated. Only love and love reciprocated can grow together and mature.

Mars is also the father of Harmonia, the most beautiful daughter of Venus, in whom wildness and gentleness, desire and pleasure unite in perfect harmony. It was she whom King Cadmus received as his wife after he had served Mars.

In Greece, Ares, as the god of war and battle, remained an

anonymous power. Individual qualities are revealed only in the few personal encounters of which there are reports, mostly concerning his relationship with Aphrodite. In the Roman world, Mars was venerated above all as the god of war and later also as a vegetation god.

Mars Viewed Psychologically

If we attempt to grasp Mars's qualities as projections of our psyche, we can be seized by fear and terror at the destructive powers in the human soul—as they have already seized us in experiencing the events of our times, in which Mars appears to be eminently at work.

The energy potential that Mars embodies is turned toward the negative by the fact that, from the very beginning, he met with a lack of understanding and rejection (Hera). Ares—etymologically, the harmer or injurer—harms himself and harms almost all those he meets. Restlessness, hate, aggression, and undefined destructive rage are the result of untamed tensions that can be inherent in a person but which become intensified due to deficient (maternal) attention. Jupiter's loyalty alone makes Mars more comprehensible, more human, as it were. By not rejecting his son but keeping him in sight—that is, by holding him in his consciousness—Jupiter was able to preserve his rights: it was not permitted to deprive him of his sanctified natural power, his dragon strength, unpunished. Cadmus had to serve him; that is, we must pay Ares his tribute, "as servants" we must become familiar with his essence so that we can alter our attitude as did King Cadmus.

It is impossible to ignore our Mars aspects, to "repress" them, to deny them their dragon power. They arise hundredfold as our shadow. And if we ourselves cannot see these shadows, our companions must suffer these sides even more intensely and clearly. Only a conscious *Auseinandersetzung* with the Mars in us can take us further. But that takes time. King Cadmus served one, four, eight long years.

For King Cadmus, the reward for his laborious *Auseinandersetzung* with Mars was Mars's daughter, Harmonia, the fruit of Mars's and Venus's loving intimacy, a successful uniting of extreme opposites. (But here, too, not every one can attain the goal. Mars has other children: "Fear" and "Terror.")

The dragon's teeth sowed on the field of Mars could be

only a multiplication of old aggressions. When Cadmus laboriously struggles and comes to terms with the Mars principle and becomes better acquainted with its positive possibilities—self-assertion, the ability to follow through, the drive to action, initiative, the urge for harmonious completion and for understanding and love—the old aggressions are overcome. They cancel each other out. The remaining five, the ancestral heroes of Thebes, are the quintessence of the martial spirit of conflict: no longer blind destructive rage, but heroism that is directed toward the future.

Mars Viewed Astrologically

Likewise astrologically, Mars is associated with two groups of meanings, negative and positive: aggression, violence, restlessness, pugnacity, drive, desire, *Sturm und Drang*, attack, intensity, etc., but also initiative, vigor and strength, enterprise, the urge and energy for deeds, desire and ardor for love, the drive to conquer, procreative power, impulse, resolve and energy, etc. In themselves, all these qualities are value-free. They acquire a positive or negative value only through the manner in which they are used or the goal that they serve; that is, through the context in which they are experienced.

Movement Tendencies

The course of the planet and his light mirror the essence—or support the projections—that are ascribed to Mars. His light alternates between a faint twinkling to a glowing red. His course is similarly inconstant: sometimes he moves more rapidly than befits his orbit time; then he is overtaken by the Sun and, to our eyes, appears to stand still. But this is no rest-taking; rather it is a tension-laden intermediate condition preceding a sudden change in the direction of action. Now he rushes toward the Sun, turns "retrograde," his light becomes weaker, until he finally changes his direction again, now moving with the Sun, as though he wanted to commence the battle or the contest anew.

Corresponding to the planet's external course, we can see the intrapsychic movement propensities that are associated with the effective power of the Mars symbol. His is always a movement that is impulsive, irregular, insistent. It exists, as it were, under pressure, tensed, comparable to the arrow on the taut bow: quickly released, it can hit the mark or soar beyond the target; al-

ways it is tensed anew, in motion once more. The movement of
Mars opposes that of Saturn: it presses outward, thrusts and
bursts, while the latter contracts, condenses. Movements with a
Mars accent are stabbing, thrusting, penetrating, intruding, ana-
lyzing, wounding, gushing forth. Mars is energy in movement; he
is initiative, impulse, drive. If the goal is specific, the movement is
directed; or it can be indefinite, and then Mars manifests as passive aggression that finds expression in unconscious urgency and
drivenness.

Sometimes in "blind rage" one cannot even see the goal, or
one takes razor-sharp aim, analyzes, and strikes. The goal may be
an external object, a person or a theme, or it can lie within oneself. Depending on the developmental level of the inner Mars, his
desire is inconstant, undirected, driven, impersonal, destructive,
or harnessed, goal-directed and solicitous, whether it be rage or
the spirit of battle that drives him, drive or initiative, aggression
or intention.

A Dream

The following dream shows how the ancient image of Mars still
today takes shape in the human soul.

> *I see a strong, young man "armed to the teeth." On closer
> inspection I see that this "armor" is a close fitting, appar-
> ently impenetrable plastic skin that, above all, outlines his
> youthful, strong body. It reveals all the strength in him.
> Shards of glass, like window glass, large and small,
> sharp and pointed, are stuck between his teeth. He
> gropes toward his mouth—and panic anxiety seizes him.*

Here the dream breaks off. Whether in his panic the man devas-
tates himself or another, or whether he encounters someone who
recognizes the danger and is able to help him remains open.

The dream shows the helplessness of a seemingly aggres-
sive "hero." Indeed, his armor, his close-fitting plastic skin, out-
lines his physical strength in a supposedly challenging manner;
but it does not let him breathe, and it can expose him more than
protect him. The shards of glass stuck between his teeth reveal
his cutting, wounding, glib tongue which is supposed to awaken
fear. But on closer inspection, one recognizes that he himself is
threatened. This hero can indeed inflict wounds, but he is in danger of cutting himself when he does so. He cannot eat, cannot

nourish himself, because he can neither chew nor digest. Here aggressions can be only poorly worked through, digested. He cannot remove the glass slivers himself because he cannot see them. Panic fear seizes him, for the splinters of glass signify his own death.

Here once again we see in concise form the essential features of the Mars myth: the turbulent, pretentious daredeviltry that often is intended only to conceal helplessness.

Destruction always also means self-destruction: whatever I annihilate outside of myself, I cannot recognize, comprehend, or bear in myself, let alone change. A person's "sharp tongue" is unpleasant to those around him but is most destructive to himself. Pure aggression is only one expression of the power Mars represents. It is all the more necessary to develop more subtle forms of Mars qualities and, above all, to achieve a comprehensive view of all the energies latent in an individual—for example, as they are mirrored in the natal horoscope. Viewed holistically, Mars, as a vital principle, most decidedly has a place in the interplay of forces.

Mars
Book of Planets, 1553

Only an unintegrated Mars attacks the order of life. Accepted by Jupiter, he finds peace, comes to his senses in Olympus, and can help in maintaining the order of life; he can generate life.

Today we would perhaps call a Mars "narcissistically disturbed." And in all persons there are mothers who reject him; on the other hand, fathers like Jupiter, who do not exactly love him as part of themselves but nevertheless accept him, are rare. And comforting Venus must turn her attention to him again and again. He is after her; he is directed to her; through her, as the complementary principle, he is redeemed.

Aphrodite (Venus)

In connection with the myths of origins, it is reported how foam arose when Saturn cast Uranus's male member behind him into the sea. Aphrodite grew up in this foam. When she was fully grown, she came to land in Cyprus. Scarcely had she touched the ground when fresh green grass sprang up, and the earth blossomed under her feet.

Animals followed her, the tame and the wild. Aphrodite is the goddess of nature in full blossom. In Lucretius we read: "When spring days appear . . . first the birds of the air, oh Goddess, announce your approach, seized in their hearts by your power; then the wild animals dance through luxuriant meadows and swim rushing streams: Thus each, gripped by magic, follows wherever Thou lead'st; in the sea, in the mountains, in wild rivers, in the foliage-shrouded dwellings of the birds, and in the green of the fields Thou fillest all hearts with sweet love and cause them ardently to propagate themselves" (in Otto 1956, p. 96). Aphrodite, therefore, is also the goddess of love and of procreative life.

Homer describes Aphrodite as the daughter of Zeus and Dione, one of the daughters of Oceanus (Homer *Iliad* 5.370). Her sacred tree is the oak, in which lustful doves make their nests. Whether as foam-born or as granddaughter of Oceanus: "It is the same magnificence that pours forth its divine magic over the sea. Peaceful seas and happy voyage bear witness to her divinity" (Otto 1956, p. 89). As sea goddess, Aphrodite causes the billows to come to rest and the waves to be calm. Now the sea is full of life and no longer "barren," as it was when Gaia gave birth to it (*Theogony* 131).

When Aphrodite sets foot on land for the first time, she is received by the goddesses of charm, the Graces. She remains most intimately linked with them and with the Horae, the goddesses of the seasons. She dances with them, and they bathe, anoint, and clothe her exquisitely. She is called "bliss of men and gods" and "lover of laughter" (*Theogony* 989).

To her, Hesiod recounts, fall the lot of "the whispering together of girls, the smiles and deceptions, the delight, and the sweetnesses of love, and the flattery" (*Theogony* 205–206). The "lover of laughter" is also called Philommedea "because she appeared from *medea*, members" (*Theogony* 200). Creative source and gentle charm, easy communication, small talk and intimate surrender, bliss of gods and men—this is Venus.

Venus/Aphrodite is invoked before weddings; likewise when a widow or widower wants to marry again. She makes hearts burst into flame for each other and imparts love its charm.

Aphrodite, so we are told, possessed a magic girdle that filled everyone with love for her who wore it. Only infrequently would she decide to loan it to another goddess, although she was

Venus and Her Children
Woodcut by Hans Sebald Beham, ca. 1530

often asked. Even Hera borrowed Aphrodite's girdle when she wanted to seduce Zeus. She herself lacked the physical charm that Aphrodite possessed in excess. Otherwise Hera, as guardian of marriage, was not well disposed to the goddess of the arts of love and seduction, not even when it was a matter of marriage or begetting children.

Even Athena was hostile to Aphrodite. When she caught Aphrodite weaving one day, she forbade her this handiwork, of which Athena was the patron goddess. Athena, Hestia (the goddess of the home and of the hearth fire), and Artemis (the goddess of the hunt) were the only ones who never let themselves be seduced by Aphrodite for any purpose. Otherwise, Aphrodite was able to bind together, bring together, or seduce any who were separated, even the most reluctant. The most impressive example of this is her intense and deep relationship with Mars, her opposite and counterpart: balance and natural grace united with restlessness and pugnacity. But her marriage with Hephaestus also reveals a union of opposites: the light-footed beauty bound herself to the limping ugly duckling and remained with him because he loved and needed her as his "better half" and could even forgive her for not belonging to him alone.

Aphrodite is love, the force that binds together and completes. She is the wealth that gives itself, that does not become poorer in giving but rather more abundant. She does not take possession. She is delight, passion, and sensual joy. Everything that appears charming—be it in form, gesture, speech, or act— bears her luster. Poets invoke her to impart "immortal charm" to their works. She can lead one to the bliss of tasting, seeing, hearing, and feeling—in art and in life.

Aphrodite/Venus is connected with nature, animals and plants, natural growth. She can enter into the spirit of the simple needs of life: girls' idle talk, laughter, caresses. She devotes herself to outer and inner beauty: to the pleasures of the senses and to inner sensibility. Her effect is without intention, free of calculation, and therefore bestowed as a gift. She loves the god of war, she loves her smith, she loves the simple shepherd Anchistes, she loves Hermes and Poseidon. She leads Paris and Helen together, unconcerned with any consequences, even those involving the god of war.

But in this goddess, too, there is a dark side, something abysmal, where her true power is first revealed. As much as one may take her grace and charm for granted, and as enticing and desired as her gifts are, one must also pay her adequate attention, gratitude, and admiration. She can be wild and destructive to any who refuse her tribute. Woe to them who do not meet her properly or who dare disdain her: she will entice them from one inordinate desire to another and sow jealousy, discord, envy, and ill will. She can provoke unquenchable longing and drive the brokenhearted mad. Wherever she is excluded or, worse, rejected as the principle of love and life, she turns the situation into its opposite and swears revenge and death.

The myth of Hippolytus attests this. This son of Theseus and of an Amazon was a friend of Artemis and therefore despised Aphrodite/Venus. He loved only manly qualities, the heroic battle, the chase, and killing. So the principle of love reversed itself: Venus caused him to fall immortally in love with Phaedra, his stepmother. Thus Aphrodite forced him to his ruin through a mother figure who could be neither his mother nor his lover. He desired an unattainable goal because he had withdrawn from Venus, the feminine love principle, from love and devotion. The goddess took her revenge on him with all sorts of further intrigues and thereby gained the help of Poseidon/Neptune, who finally caused Hippolytus's own horse to drag him to death. Thus Hippolytus's excessively masculine driving force, his "horsepower," ultimately ruins him.

Not only men but women, too, must be in tune with Venus and grant her the rank which is her due lest they share the fate of the king's daughter, Myrrha. Myrrha was beautiful but also very vain and believed her own hair more beautiful than Venus's. Myrrha was punished: she was compelled to fall hopelessly in love with her own father. When he found out that she was pregnant by him, he pursued her with his sword. At that point, Venus quickly transformed her into a myrrh tree. When her father pierced it, the youth Adonis, Myrrha's child, sprang forth.

Whenever a woman is not in tune with the Venus principle, if she closes herself to Venus or wants to compete with her—i.e., if she does not serve Venus or is not thankful for her workings, but is "headstrong" and turns her hair, her thoughts, against Venus—her womanly surrender and devotion becomes perverted. She remains infantile, bound to the father principle and to a patriarchal world; she is full of hate or in flight from this world.

In Venus herself, light and dark sides battle for preeminence. This is shown not only in her strongly differing tendencies, but also in her internal conflict over Adonis, Myrrha's son. Initially Venus did not know what to make of him; she put him in a chest and gave him to Persephone, the goddess of the underworld. When she later saw what a beautiful youth and lover he had grown to be, she wanted to contest Persephone's right to him. The decision stipulated that Adonis was to spend one third of the year with Aphrodite/Venus and one third with Persephone, but for the remaining third he was to be free. Venus then seduced him to tarry longer with her. Thus she entangled her youthful lover in a conflict between the goddess of love and nature and the goddess of the dark and the underworld. Jupiter was not willing to settle this dispute; he left the judgment to the Muse Calliope, so it had to be settled by the feminine principle itself in its various aspects.

Again, the essence of this divinity encompasses the full range: light and dark, love and destruction, depending on how one approaches her, which side one addresses in her.

Venus Viewed Psychologically

Psychologically, as astrologically, Venus is to be regarded as the function of relationship. Possibilities of relationship on various levels are embodied in her image. Like all planetary functions or archetypal forces, Venus works equally in men and in women. She causes the striving for completion in all that is incomplete.

For a man, Venus is the complementary feminine component in him (in Jungian parlance: the anima) under a certain aspect. (We shall meet further facets of this feminine component in connection with the moon.) For a woman, Venus belongs to her female identity, whose complement is the masculine.

Venus is a life principle that no one can deny with impunity. Hippolytus disavowed the feminine principle in himself and was punished with a fatal one-sidedness. Similar things can happen to a woman who does not find her way to her feminine identity.

Venus strives for balance. She can work introvertedly as well as extravertedly. She brings the individual into relationship with oneself and into harmony with one's counterpart, intrapsychically as well as externally, where she establishes relationship to people and to the world.

Wherever Venus is strong, Mars cannot overpower as an inner quality (as animus, in Jungian terminology) nor as a partner. Two equally strong forces meet and bring forth something new. New life is born when two are "joined . . . in love through golden Aphrodite" (*Theogony* 1004–1005).

Venus awakens delight in the senses, establishes a relation between inner and outer nature. She makes possible communication on all levels, in all realms: through hearing, seeing, smelling, touching, tasting.

In hearing, euphony or diaphony is perceived, in the voice of mother, the friend, the beloved. Moods are awakened, and attunement to each other, which may be unison and harmony, or discord, dissension, dissonance.

In seeing, we take the world into ourselves. Inner and outer images are linked and create the atmosphere or mood of our contact with the world.

Smells evoke feelings of well-being and awaken memories, but also displeasure. A certain taste is distinct and permeates the surroundings, the clothes one wears, the books one reads. Venus is at work.

The most immediate way to come into relationship with something is through touch. The infant grasps what is closest; we seize the world about us and attempt to comprehend it. To savor our feelings, to be seized with emotion, to be enthused—all are paraphrases of Venus functions.

To seize and to be seized signify emotion: one is moved and, accordingly, moves in conformity with mood in gait, expression, and demeanor.

Venus can manifest in the entire range from the simplest form to the most highly perfected figure; from the simplest reference to a thing or theme to a work of art; from the simplest human contact to the fulfillment of the deepest passions of love.

All relation to the world and all contact with our fellow human beings is possible due to our senses, regardless of the level to which the perception is subsequently linked and the relationship seen. The myths of Venus reveal a broad spectrum of her possible workings, her function.

Venus Viewed Astrologically

Astrologically, Venus is associated with good fellowship, enjoyment, esthetics, pleasure, luxury, and the delights and arts of love; with art in general, with beauty, play, and the pleasures of the senses; with a sense of proportion and harmony; with the strivings for balance and completion, harmony and a sense of well being.

Movement Tendencies

Many qualities that one experiences in the symbol of Venus are mirrored in the planet's course.

Venus's art of binding opposites together is reflected, for example, in the fact that Venus can be at one time the luminous evening star and at another time the brightest of the morning stars. From bright day she casts her light into the night, and out of the darkness she beams into day, uniting and binding together bright and dark, day and night.

The light of Venus is calm and warm; of all the planets, her course is the most symmetrical (since her trajectory is almost circular).From early on she was regarded as the star of balance and harmony.

People were able to measure time and calculate the length of the year from her orbit. These qualities attained special importance when certain laws of number were discovered. The orbit of Venus and her position in regard to the earth and to the sun revealed numerical proportions that corresponded to those of the golden mean, that proportion which has been regarded as the essence of the harmonious and which has been demonstrated in art whenever a work has been experienced as particularly harmonious and beautiful. For harmonious proportions in the macrocosm or in the visible world correspond to similar ones in the microcosm or in the human psyche.

If we sketch the positions of the lesser conjunctions of Venus and the Sun in the zodiac, we obtain a pentagram which, since the time of Pythagoras, has been regarded as a sign of good luck (Xylander 1971, p. 67).[9]

Harmony, warmth, and happiness are the experiential qualities that correspond symbolically to Venus. As psychic tendencies, we could mention connecting, bringing together, uniting, moving, fulfilling, giving, gifting, flowing, seducing, resonating, creating proper proportion, bringing into relationship, etc. Charm, cheerfulness, and bliss are the graces that accompany Venus.

But this still holds true: no psychic force, no planetary symbol, stands alone and independent. Each experiences the most varied inflections and shadings depending on the context in which it is situated.

A Dream

In the following dream, Venus herself was not visibly present, but
it seems to me that she was nevertheless everywhere at work
here, invisibly.

> *A warm summer day. On the garden fence, blackberry*
> *canes with delicious berries: half like pomegranates, half*
> *plump berries. In a bed close by grow tomato plants with*
> *splendid red round fruits and dark green rich leaves, like*
> *I have never seen. (When I was a child, tomatoes were*
> *called "paradises," paradise apples.)*
>   *A feast begins. Friends come bringing gifts: salt*
> *and pepper in magnificent cut glass containers on an em-*
> *bossed silver tray, a delight for the eye and spice for life*
> *at the same time. As a surprise, young girls in the kitchen*
> *have already done the cooking. Many are sitting together*
> *outside on the grass, which children had cut earlier and*
> *which is strewn with colorful cushions, enjoying the deli-*
> *cious food.*
>   *A drink, brought by an older woman, is passed*
> *around: one small swallow suffices to create the most*
> *magnificent feeling of well-being. Great, red currants are*
> *lying on a white coverlet in the sunshine.*
>   *Then we hear music: children and a few grown-*
> *ups climb out the windows of the neighboring houses and*
> *play on stringed instruments and flutes. One man has*
> *made a bagpipe from a teapot and plays it most artfully.*
> *The procession winds through the streets. Where to?*

Euphony, pleasant tastes, fruits, love potion, girls' chatter, sweet
rapture, embraces and caresses—here the dream gives form to
the divine honors of Venus, perhaps almost too beautiful for some
who would prefer more drama. The shadow side is absent, since
Venus works her spell without a counterpart or envier, but also
without her complement.

Hermes (Mercury)

Mercury is the planet closest to the sun and of all the gods perhaps the closest to man. Mercury plays a role in almost all
human endeavors and mediates among all, just as in myth he
was the mediator among heaven, earth, and the underworld, messenger of the gods and guide to humankind.
    Hermes/Mercury is a son of Zeus and the nymph Maia.[10]

The Homeric hymn to Hermes recounts how he was secretly begotten and born in her cave on Mount Mykene. But from the beginning, the exceptional divine element in him was obvious. In the hymn, it is said, "Then she gave birth to a baby, devious, wily, a robber, a rustler of cattle, a dream guide—yes, the conductor of dreams—and a spy in the night—and a lookout skulking at other men's doors. . . . Born in the morning, by noon he was playing the zither, by nightfall he had abducted the cattle belonging to marksman Apollo," his brother, who overshadowed him (Hine 1972, p. 32).

Already, the first day, he escaped from his swaddling clothes and leaped over the threshold of the house. There he found a tortoise and immediately seized it. "I shall not deplore you! . . . .but first you shall serve me" (ibid.). With swift and purposeful hand, he takes the tortoise's shell and adroitly constructs from it a musical instrument, the lyre, on which he also immediately can play absolutely magnificently, so that later he is able to soften and enchant Apollo's heart with it but also cut a favorable deal with him.

Then it is told how, on his adventures, he discovers Apollo's cattle and immediately steals all fifty. He devises a stratagem: he has the cattle walk backward and makes for himself "shoes" of twigs and grass so that no one can recognize his footprints and all traces will be obliterated. Thus, in darkness, he drives the cattle backward into a cave.

There he slaughters two cattle as an offering, butchers and roasts them, and makes twelve piles of meat. As he does this, he resists the temptation to taste the delicious roast and carefully observes all the customs of sacrifice.

Then he hurries home, slips back into his swaddling clothes, and lies curled up in his cradle like an innocent, little baby. Early the next morning, when Apollo comes to look after his herd, he can find it nowhere and looks for a long time in vain. Finally, an old shepherd sends him to Hermes. Apollo threatens to throw his brother into Tartaros if he does not take him to his cattle. But Hermes says, "What is the meaning of these cruel words, son of Leto, you utter? Is it in search of your pastoral cattle you pay us this visit? I have not seen them nor learned of them from the report of another. . . .an infant newborn who has passed the courtyard with cows from the field? You are making extravagant charges!" (Hine 1972, p. 30).

Apollo takes Hermes before Zeus, accuses him of theft, and demands justice. Hermes denies it: "You will believe me: you

Hermes and His Children
Woodcut by Hans Sebald Beham, ca. 1530

boast that you are my affectionate father! I haven't driven his cattle to my house . . . nor—I declare this with certainty—did I step over the threshold" (ibid., p. 41). His oath is not entirely false, for he had jumped across the threshold and hid the cattle in the cave, not in the house. Zeus cannot be angry with his youngest son. He "laughed aloud when he saw how his mischievous infant well and expertly denied that he knew anything about cattle" (ibid.). Hermes notes that he has already won halfway, and finally, in response to Apollo's insistence, is ready to take him to the cattle. "You can have your herds again. I slaughtered only two animals and divided them in twelve parts, as offerings for the twelve gods." "Twelve gods?" Apollo asks. "Who is the twelfth?" "Your servant, Lord" (Ranke-Graves 1960, p. 53). Thus, Hermes smuggles himself into Olympus; but later Zeus himself installs him there with all honors.

When Apollo sees the slaughtered, skinned, and butchered beef, he is astonished. "How did you manage to do it? to skin these two heifers? a newborn baby, an infant, as you are, however deceitful and cunning? Much I admire your strength when I think of it! There is no need . . . for you to grow bigger" (ibid., p. 42).

Apollo wants to bind Hermes, but Hermes can free himself magically. Then he takes out his lyre, plays upon it, and sings bewitchingly, beautifully. With intentionally self-serving words, he praises the immortal gods and Apollo's honor. But the music so grips Apollo in his heart of hearts that he breaks out in "divine laughter." Hermes gives him the lyre and in exchange receives Apollo's golden staff. Apollo also appoints Hermes as master over all Apollo's cattle herds and teaches him everything he needs to know about it. Hermes/Mercury promises never to steal the lyre nor any of his other possessions. Now Apollo calls him "gold staff brother" and "beloved" and himself takes Hermes again to Olympus and tells Zeus all that has happened. "Zeus's thoughtfulness rejoiced as he looked upon" the inventive, eloquent, and convincing little god. "Make me your messenger, Father," Hermes says, and promises to attend to the security of all divine possessions and never again to lie. But he cannot promise always to tell the whole truth. Thereupon, Zeus entrusts to him the guardianship of all contracting, promotion of trade, and maintenance of the rights of way for all travelers on all the roads of the world. Additionally, Zeus gives him the round cap to protect against the rain and the winged, golden sandals that carry him everywhere with the speed of the wind. From Hades he gets the cloak of invisibility so that he can appear anywhere unseen.

Everyone in the Olympian family was glad to accept Hermes, and he served them all. He saved the yet unborn Dionysus and sewed him inside Zeus's thigh so that Zeus could carry him the three remaining months until his birth. It was Hermes who helped Aries/Mars escape from the prison in which he had been held for ten years, where he was about to die. He was Hades's messenger and "summoned" the souls of the dying by gently laying his staff on their eyes so that the golden luster escorted them down into the underworld.

With the golden staff, Hermes can plunge one into sleep but also awaken. He brings dreams and guides persons awake as well as asleep. "Companion of Dreams" was his nickname. He guides souls, without reward, without demanding compensation.

Hermes did have the ambition to belong to the Olympians, yet he was not concerned with power or fame. In the *Iliad*, he says that Leto should go ahead and boast that she vanquished him with her strength; he preferred to avoid further conflict with her. When Hephaestus captures Aries and Aphrodite in his finely spun net as they embrace and exposes them to the derision of the gods, Hermes admits that he would have liked to lie beside Aphrodite as much as Aries did, even if there were three times as many nets and all the goddesses looked on disapprovingly. (Later, he attained his pleasure, without spectators, and begat the hermaphrodite.)

Hermes is also the god of merchants and artisans. Odysseus says to Eumaios, the swineherd, that all people have Hermes to thank when "grace and fame" accompany their works, even those of so simple a nature as his.

Hermes is rooted to no single place; he is always underway. As god of roads and right-of-way, he finds the suitable path for each—and not always a straight and narrow one. Himself a thief, he protects thieves and highwaymen.

The many herms found everywhere refer to him: rectangular, also phallic, stones or stelas erected in front of houses as apotropaic magic and as protection from thieves, or piles of stones at the side of the road to which each passerby reverently added a stone in remembrance of the guide and with the request for his favor.

Hermes/Mercury never works his effects by force but rather by means of friendly exhortation, cunning, eloquence and versatility, good intuitions, and magic (or he helps against magic, as when he gives Odysseus a healing herb to counter Circe's magic). Good with words, a trait revealed in infancy, Hermes became the god of language, both spoken and written word. He is reputed to have helped the goddesses of fate invent the alphabet.

Mercury Viewed Psychologically

Like Ares, Mercury embodies a certain side of Jupiter, who "secretly" loved Maia, "secretly" begat Mercury, and thereby "deceived" Hera. These are qualities that his son represents in rich measure. But again, Jupiter acknowledges this potential in himself and receives Mercury into the circle of gods on Olympus, just as he also accepted Mars. They all represent individual functions in the overall structure of his world order.

Jupiter cannot resist Mercury's particular charm, his adroitness, his seemingly childlike lack of inhibition, his great gifts of inventiveness, skill, and diligence. He "rejoices in his heart" that two so very different brothers have made a heartfelt peace.

As entertaining or refreshing as the tales of Mercury are, and as much as one may delight in identifying with him in his successful knavery, many nevertheless sometimes feel rather uncomfortable. One cannot take completely unmixed pleasure in his masterful playing of the lyre and his bewitching song: while Apollo is profoundly gripped and animated by this music, Mercury cultivates "advantageous" thoughts and follows calculated plans.

One can stand close to or far from Mercury, depending on one's native endowment. But what everybody finds lacking at times in the figure of Mercury are feelings, depth, *Innerlichkeit.*

Let us once more consider his various qualities as they are presented in the Homeric hymn. Mercury is mobile and enterprising. He seizes the moment and what it offers, full of inventiveness. One can only marvel at him—just as Apollo did. Not everyone who sees something—a tortoise, for example—can make something of it. Not everybody is given to kill an animal with resolve and self-assurance and to disembowel it, even if it is advantageous or serves higher purposes.

Mercury steals, but not to possess. People can forgive him. He wants honor, but he is not concerned with power. Indeed, he serves without recompense, for free. That is a quality people value, especially today when it is so very hard to find. He is fearless, but he does not have much to lose, either. He is friendly and ready to help—everyone, unfortunately.

Mercury invents the instruments or means, but not the contents that they serve, for example, the musical instrument, but it is Apollo who brings the spirit and the soul of music. Mercury provides the language, the possibility of logical thought, but he is not concerned with the truth or with deep meaning. He sends dreams, but not their interpretation, not the meanings to which they might point.

In pursuing his goals, his purposes, he can deceive, indeed mystify, an intensification of the art of producing illusions. It can be distressing when he feigns or consciously employees feelings (for example, his divine song) and is not emotionally engaged but rather thinking advantageously.

Here, if not sooner, the uneasiness that occasionally seizes us when we encounter purely mercurial functions begins to grow, whether the functions appear in ourselves or in others. We become suspicious of certain motivations: Is it calculation? Bribery? Persuasiveness? Avaricious striving without any sense of higher values?

This sort of discomfort appears whenever we are involved exclusively and in the extreme with any function that, so to speak, has become autonomous. We can feel very much the same with the urgent drives of Mars or the overwhelming sensuality of Venus.

While we were closer to or farther from specific qualities in regard to the other functions, it seems as though Mercury lacks his own unique qualities: he is capable of, does, and is everything in all areas. He has neither preference nor antipathy; he is value-free. To this extent, he is "unethical." There is no divine figure, no function, that can accommodate itself with such supple flattery to whatever it meets, adapt and hence be so "charming."

But this also means that Mercury always needs a counterpart if he is to attain the full flowering of his magic. Where Venus's grace is spontaneous and natural, Mercury employs his magic and his art of mediation consciously. Hence, in Mercury's case, it is of special significance who his counterpart or companion is, who he serves. Apollo can exalt him as his "golden staffed brother" who guides souls and directs dreams. But vis-à-vis a thief, Mercury is the master thief, and with a highwayman he is an intrigant.

It also depends on one's talents or abilities—and on one's values—as to what sort of companion he is. The form and the quality of Mercury's mediation and how he exercises his effects depends on the goals and the qualities of the other functions within. His lack of values or his willingness to serve all has the advantage that no collusions, battles, or wars come about through his agency; rather, he attempts to hinder these sorts of things. He is always diplomatic. Mercury, in a sense, has no character of his own, but a unique ability which he puts at our disposal. On Olympus—or in the human soul—the various forces so turbulently battle with each other that there is need of an adroitly calculating, soberly negotiating, clever negotiator as value-free as possible. That is Mercury.

Mercury Viewed Astrologically

In astrology, Mercury's close proximity to the Sun and hence the weakness of its own light, its own "lack of uniqueness," is always mentioned as the feature that makes Mercury the mediator, the messenger among the other powers. Be it due to its orbit, to ancient astrological tradition, or to experience, certain associations have always clung to Mercury: sobriety, calculation, agility, precision, tactics, technique, pragmatism, versatility, realism, intelligence, conceptual ability, routine, self-interest, eloquence, etc. These terms attempt to "translate" the symbolic images, and they also serve an imaginal representation themselves.

Mercury
Book of Planets, 1553

Movement Tendencies

The same thing happens when we visualize Mercury's movement tendencies. The "hasty course" of the planet, which appears to scurry hither and thither, now ahead, now after the Sun, first setting, then rising before, corresponds to the psychological movement of the psychopomp, "being always underway," always on the move. Perpetually being in motion (not being moved in the sense of emotion or feeling) mirrors today's peculiar widespread inclination not to rest or to hurry where one has no time for anything sensible, for oneself, for example. It corresponds to the desire, indeed the addiction, to travel, to scurry from one undertaking to another, from one continent to another, always with improvements.

The rootless quality in Mercury himself allows him to join company with every fellow traveler. All our activities have perhaps the same background: fewer and fewer people have deep roots, be it in the family, in the community, in their native land, or in intellectual or religious contexts. People move into apartment communities, try their luck in various relationships, link up with all possible sorts of special interest groups, and are always going somewhere, searching for a lucky find (*Konios* in Greek). In ancient Greece, "Konios Hermes" was the watchword of every business venture. With this expression, people wished each other "Common discovery and prey!" Today, we say "Good luck!"

Likewise the tendency to talk a lot but not always to tell the truth corresponds to the mercurial movement tendency. The many words, facts, books—the expanded alphabet of the goddesses of fate—reflect Mercury in their ever faster circulation in our times. "Disguised"—that is, unbeknownst to us—Mercury is on the move and at work where we do not even suspect him. Wherever we grasp, conceptualize, take up, work through, mediate, Mercury is present. Likewise, he is there when we make available our psychic resources, introduce, or accompany.

Mercury is the guide of souls, demanding no recompense. From us, he receives no thanks, even if we make constant use of his assistance. Even for the dreams he sends, only few know how to be grateful. Very many people still say: I always dream only stupid stuff.

The smallest, most neutral, inconspicuous god, this "nursling" was neglected because he could conceal himself under the cloak of invisibility. He wanted to be only a messenger, a mediator, and now—at least in many manifestations of our civilization and in many persons—he has become independent, automated, computerized. Gradually he comes to mediate almost autonomously and—now barely disguised—seems to be the most powerful god of our time, this technical, scientific age with which the individual can scarcely keep up.

But in one for whom feeling for Mercury still exists, where in the soul the function mediating between conscious and unconscious contents is still alive and can be summoned in times of need, a "conversation among the gods" (i.e., among the psychic functions, the archetypes, or whatever one wishes to call them) can still take place.

A Dream

The following dream, in which some aspects of Mercury are revealed, is "mercurial" even in its external form, like a motion picture film in which several sequences have been edited close together. One image follows another like the daily news on television.

> *1) A train compartment. A conductor opens the door—and looks in inquiringly. "Any questions?"*
>
> *2) A woman has come for an astrological reading. But rather than looking at the natal horoscope, she writes as fast as the wind so that she will get all the facts, fills one page after another, and lets the finished pages fall to the floor beside her.*
>
> *3) In a street with stores. A rather seamy looking man: short, broad-shouldered, flashy suit, briefcase, but from the rear one can see that he is wearing no stockings. A heavy-set American woman dressed in loud colors is walking beside him. They are on the way to a business lunch with a banker.*
>
> *4) In a church. A cleric in a black coat and hat is standing in the pulpit and proclaiming that whoever wants to leave before communion may do so. Practically everybody leaves the church.*
>
> *5) A large train station. Very functional, but remarkably everything is art nouveau. Oval lines define all elements: windows, walls, the angle of light from above. All lines are consistently drawn (there seem to be no right angles at all); severe and supple at the same time.*

Lively—and unpleasantly moving images. The conductor (also a traveler) *would like* actually to be useful and looks almost roguishly provocative as he inquires if there isn't somebody who wants information about the trip.

In the second scene the life pattern, the natal horoscope, can be appreciated only intellectually. Data cover many sheets of paper, but everything remains superficial. The woman writes like an automaton, without any emotional investment.

The businessman in the third scene is somewhat exposed in his shoes. Perhaps he is the image of a modern thief?

The pastor is maybe all too anxious or miserly in protecting the divine property—or is this a skillful way of finding out for whom being an errand boy or psychopomp is still worthwhile?

The "modern" train station is an intersection of many paths, Mercury's field of activity.

These brief snapshots reveal Mercury in various garb: adapted or disguised, but without "lucky finds." Here, perhaps the right partner or challenger is lacking.

Sun and Moon

The Sun and the Moon occupy, in differing ways, a special place among the planets. Only by astrologers are they treated as "planets," as symbols of parts or powers in the soul. Regarded astronomically they are, of course, not planets.

But all times and all cultures have experienced them as representatives of two fundamental psychic principles. As the celestial bodies of day and night, they are still today symbols, even when we are occupied with them in a seemingly matter-of-fact way. In regard to the Sun and the Moon, is it obvious that our life is influenced, indeed shaped, physically, psychically, and socially by these bodies.

Day and night form the foundation of our vital rhythm and of our activity. The alternation of light and dark, from day to day, from year to year, shapes our personal and social life. The effects of this alternation on organic and social life and the possibilities that arise as a result have been researched as subjects in physics, biology, and sociology. But to a great extent, the effects on our psyche, our emotional reaction, lie beyond the reach of our causal-rational grasp. The Sun and the Moon remain symbols.

Each planet that we have considered so far embraced polarities when seen against the mythical background: "positive" and "negative" qualities. The Sun and the Moon—the celestial bodies of day and of night—designate once again the most extreme opposites, such as light and dark, sky and earth, masculine and feminine principles, yin and yang, or the Chinese glyphs (from the *I Ching*) for Ch'ien, the creative, and K'un, the receptive:

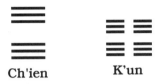

Ch'ien   K'un

Every person is shaped by both principles—or essential energies—everyone participates in them. The masculine and the feminine principles are present in both sexes, they are represented in each horoscope, men and women are equally endowed with them, and, whether consciously or unconsciously, every person experiences these energies as specific strivings and experiential qualities. The more consciousness one brings to this and the more successful one is in letting both principles flower, the more complete or fulfilled will be one's experience of one's personality and life.

What especially impresses us about the Sun and the Moon is their life and their course that determine the cycles of day and night, month and year. But they still differ fundamentally in this. The course of the Moon impresses us by its rapid cycle of changing phases—new, waxing, full, and waning moon—which recurs ever and again. In the Sun's course, it is the constant rhythm of day and night and the rhythm of the year, the primordial image of the entire course of a life or of life's rhythm.

Cyclical return belongs to the essence of the mythical. Very different symbols derive from the differing effective powers and the various external manifestations of the Sun and Moon symbols.

The Moon stands in closer relationship to myth, in close proximity to images from the unconscious, images that revolve around the various aspects of the feminine principle. The experience of the Sun symbol has, as we shall see, led to images that stand closer to consciousness, such as are represented most impressively in the signs of the zodiac.

Moon

Since time immemorial and still today, the Moon is associated with "the receptive" in astrological tradition and in psychological interpretation: with perceptive openness and the resulting readiness to react, to respond. In Chinese the glyph K'un stands for "the receptive": receptive devotion and surrender. "The Receptive in its riches carries all things. Its nature is in harmony with the boundless. It embraces everything in its breadth and illumines everything in its greatness. Through it, all individual being attain success" (*I Ching*, p. 386). In the realm of emotions, K'un refers to the condition of receptive openness to life and to the world.

Part of our fundamental existential situation lies in our embeddedness in the "abundance of all things," in boundless riches or (in psychological parlance) in the collective unconscious in which the plenitude of all the possibilities of human experiencing are contained.

In the life of the individual, this corresponds to the condition of the child that is still completely contained in the mother. Individual experiences and developments are differentiated out of this embeddedness: "individual beings" appear, they are born. The image for this process of growth and maturation is contained in the symbol of the Moon, in the interplay of Moon and Earth and in the cycles of the Moon's phases. The Moon's phases, for their part, mirror the essence of the "feminine principle" in its various aspects, an essence that can be experienced in all areas of human life.

The Moon has always moved the human soul and evoked the most varied responses in myth, tale, legend, cult and rite, in custom, art, magic, and sorcery. Vastly different notions coexist side by side and at the same time in the same person: the experience of changeability stands beside the hope of the reliable return of the familiar.

The essence of the Moon symbol can be comprehended best on the basis of its motions and the movement tendencies that the Moon effects: the attraction of the Moon causes ebb and flow. The rising, surging, and sinking of water has correspondences in the organic as well as in the psychic domains. The rise and fall of sap belongs to all growth—as well as to the sexual experience of men and women.

It is repeated in women's monthly cycle, which mirrors the Moon's cycle: new moon, full moon, waning moon, and dark of the moon find their correspondences in the preparation and engorgement of the lining of the uterus, in the release of the ovum (which, if it is fertilized, could bring into being woman's full fruit), and finally in menstruation, in the sloughing off of the unused tissue. And scarcely has this phase run its course when the new cycle begins.

Even more impressive, the Moon cycle is experienced in conception, pregnancy, birth (full moon), nursing (waning), and finally in surrendering, in the gradual separation of the child from the mother.

Woman's biology itself is only an image (itself again a symbol) for the essence of the feminine principle or the yin. But woman and feminine principle must not be equated.

The yin is inherent in all living things. Only yin *and* yang, masculine and feminine together result in the totality of a living organism.

If we consider the symbol of the Moon, it is naturally linked with the image of the feminine, and it is not surprising that all myths or mythical figures that are associated with the Moon depict aspects of the feminine.[11]

Moon Myths

There are various mythic figures associated with the various phases of the Moon, for example, Selene.

Selene

Selene is *the* Moon goddess in Greek mythology. She is the daughter of Hyperion and Thea, both Titans, "children" of Uranus and Gaia. Helios, the Sun, and Eos, the dawn, are her siblings. But Helios is also her spouse, and when she joins with him, when they share the bed, Selene is no longer to be seen: the new moon rules. This is an image of the primordial beginnings; the "receptive is in accord with the boundless."

Selene was regarded as the goddess of women in general; as the goddess of growth of plants, animals, and humans; and also as goddess of night, sleep, and death. Selene loved a youth, Endymion, one of Zeus's sons to whom his father had given eternal youth and eternal sleep. Selene, enchanted by him, visited him in sleep and gave him fifty daughters.

This tale describes *one* of the Moon's possibilities: the union with eternal youth and eternal sleep. It depicts a state of persistence in the blissful unconscious, in "pure innocence," in the purely vegetative, in self-sufficiency and self-propagation. Selene "gives" herself to Endymion ever and again and gives him

Luna and Her Children
Woodcut by Hans Sebald Beham, ca. 1530

fifty daughters, many new manifestations of herself. But Endymion could not see them, since he was asleep; hence, there is no relationship between them, no awakening and maturation. This aspect of the Moon symbol or of the "feminine principle" is plenitude that cyclically gives of itself ever and anew without, however, "individual beings coming into existence," without the awakening of consciousness and the development of differentiation.

Artemis

Artemis is later equated with Selene. Artemis is the virgin goddess of the hunt, the mistress of animals. Armed with bow and arrow, she is the "Mistress of the Outdoors." Hearth, home, and family are not her affair. She is ambivalent toward the feminine: she can slay women in childbirth, but she can also assist with birthing. The animals of the forest are closer to her heart. She herself loves to live in the open, among nymphs, youthful women who remain young and have a long life but who are not immortal. Artemis is associated with the waxing moon, for everything still lies before her.

It is easy to recognize in Artemis a feminine principle that has again become important today: Artemis is free, mistress of the animals, of living drives. What previously was possible only through chastity is now possible with birth control. Artemis hunts but does not let herself be hunted. She hates, or envies, the mothers in childbed, for in her, too, resides the wish and the possibility of having a child. But again and again, Artemis withdraws from the bonds entailed in being a mother. She is interested in roaming, not in homemaking. The young women with whom she lives remain young a long time, but they are not immortal: they no longer have the eternal youth of Endymion nor can they remain in eternal sleep, in blissful unconsciousness. They must either die without maturing, for they have not entered into life in any binding way, or their "virginity" dies; the time of the young girl is not infinite.

Hence the connection with Artemis is not an enduring condition, but rather one possibility, one facet or phase of feminine being or a mood of the soul.

Kore (Persephone)

Kore, too, was associated with Selene and, like Artemis, with the Moon in its waxing phase. Kore means "the maiden" or also "the grain maiden." Her mother is Demeter, the goddess of grain, who grants the fields their fertility. Demeter and Kore together are the goddesses of vegetative growth (as Selene is, too), but in them "growing and ripening" is especially emphasized. Kore mirrors two phases or possibilities of the "feminine principle."

Kore is a daughter of Demeter and Zeus who, "widely discerning," promised her to his brother, Hades (Pluto) (Hine 1972, p. 6). But Demeter opposes the plan. She wants to keep Kore with her. Kore is also called "the chaste one," for Demeter watches over her, always keeps her close to her, and above all does not want to surrender her to Pluto. Thus, it finally happens that Hades must abduct Kore—with Zeus's consent and while he looks on.

"When she was playing apart from her mother Demeter the golden giver of glorious fruits. . .gathering flowers, the roses and crocus that grow in the midst of deep grassy meadows as well as fair lilies and hyacinths, iris, and the narcissus, which earth at the bidding of Zeus had produced. . .a snare for the flower-faced maiden. . .a glorious hundredfold blossom. . . . The Maiden was struck with amazement, and reached out with both of her hands to seize the desirable plaything. Then earth gaped. . .the underworld offspring of Kronos leapt, with his immortal horses, straight out of the chasm upon her" (ibid., p. 4).

From now on Kore is called Persephone. No longer is she the maiden who plays and dances free of care.

For nine days, Demeter seeks her daughter and wanders over the entire Earth. On the tenth day, Hecate finally tells her that she had heard the girl screaming when she vanished. They implore the aid of Helios, who can illuminate every corner, and he tells Demeter that everything happened on Zeus's advice, "who gave her to Hades as his wife." And he consoles her that, after all, Hades is Zeus's brother, "from the same womb." But Demeter is not to be consoled; she is angry and swears never again to let anything grow on Earth if she does not get her daughter back. Later, after a long drought, she is ready to be reconciled with Hades. Zeus sends Hermes and has him ask Hades to let Persephone return to Earth again. Hades "obeyed the behest of Zeus" (Hine 1972, p. 13). But before Persephone goes, he gives her "covertly. . .a sweet pomegranate seed. . .so that she should not abide the rest of her days at the side of her mother, impressive Demeter" (ibid.). Once more he, as god of the underworld, honors her: "In this kingdom you shall be mistress of everything living and creeping and have the greatest proportion of honor among the immortals" (ibid.).

Hermes brings Persephone back to Earth. But when Demeter hears from her daughter's very own mouth that she has eaten the death food (even if only the seed of a pomegranate), she knows and accepts that Persephone can no longer return fully to Earth.

From now on, Persephone spends one-third of the year as underworld goddess with Hades and two-thirds of the year with Demeter on the earth above. Since her return, Demeter again lets the grain grow luxuriantly.

In this myth, the growth and maturation aspects occupy the foreground, in nature, in the vegetative realm, as in the psychic domain. Kore cannot remain only a maiden, only chaste. She must descend into the depths, must become Persephone, in order to bring up new riches from Hades. Seven seeds of the pomegranate she is said to have eaten: seeds for new fruit on the Earth. Cycles are perceived, understood, and accepted.

Here the clutching, devouring aspect of the mother is also revealed, that aspect which does not want to grant this sort of maturation. Demeter does not want to surrender that blissful, primordial condition of mother–infant, mother–daughter oneness. But by plucking Hades's flower, albeit with terror and delight, Kore makes it possible for him to abduct her; indeed, he *already has* abducted her. Kore becomes "Persephone," the chaste one is transformed into the mature one, and in cyclical return, new fertility becomes possible.

Zeus supports the wish of his brother from the depths to marry Zeus's earthly daughter, the daughter of earth's fullness. Union with the depths comprises part of the wholeness of the cosmic order. A symbol for this is the marriage of the daughter of heaven (Zeus) and earth (grain goddess) with the god of darkness, of the dead, and of the underworld.

In other words, it is a question of uniting the receptive, yin side of consciousness with the god of the depths and of the unconscious. (The "land of the dead" is also a synonym for the collective unconscious in which the personal unconscious is contained like a seed.)

Life and death limit one another, just as do waking and sleeping. Wherever the depths do not receive a voluntary "sacrifice," a goddess, the gaping abyss opens and what was refused is taken violently.

But in the depths there are also "sweet" fruits: pomegranates, Aphrodite's fruit, which joins what is separated and awakens desire. Whoever has eaten of the food of the dead—and especially of the sweet pomegranate—must return to the land of the dead.

69

All accept this as self-evident: Persephone, the receptive sensibility, the soul, belongs one-third to the realm of the dead. Ascent and descent follows a cyclical course. (We spend approximately one-third of our life in sleep.) Whoever has entered the cycle of life and death, waking and sleeping, must ever and again return to the depths. There, not only are the physical powers renewed; the psyche, too, receives its nourishment, the picture world of dreams.

Demeter does not want to relinquish her daughter for two reasons. It is difficult to give up something one has come to love, to renounce the rejuvenating and enlivening reflection in one's daughter. Moreover, Demeter fears the unknown, the "unnameable" (as Hades is called). Hers is the fear of consciousness at the prospect of submersion, of being devoured in the unconscious, the fear of the uncertainty and strangeness of another world, on another condition. But the world of Hades cannot be known, i.e., cannot be conscious, precisely because it belongs to the unconscious and consequently excludes consciousness. A union of these opposites is not possible, only movement back and forth from the one domain to the other, just as Persephone does.

It is part of Jupiter's marvelous world order that the connection to the depths became possible via Persephone, even if initially she did not volunteer to journey across the border between the worlds of consciousness and the unconscious. But understanding the necessity, and perhaps the meaning, she returns periodically.

Like Persephone, human beings must also periodically immerse themselves in the realm of the unconscious. We can do this, figuratively speaking, thanks to our moon function. If we do not do so willingly, we are taken there (we are "overcome" by sleep, "stricken," "taken" by death, etc.).

The food of the depths can be seductively sweet. In Hades's pomegranate we can see the complement to the apple of paradise that Eve handed to Adam, which grew on the Tree of Knowledge of Good and Evil and imparted consciousness to humankind. Hades's, or Pluto's, apple contains the sweetness that lets us return to the depths, to the darkness, to unconsciousness.

From this point of view, Paradise and Hades, heaven and underworld, have moved very close together. But the unknown beginning that lies behind us does not have the terrifying aspect of the unknown and unnameable that still lies before us and that we experience as threat and danger.

In the Moon's cycle, beginning and end have come together. The darkness of the dark moon was experienced as the
portal to the underworld. Persephone was swallowed by the gaping darkness. Through the portal of the underworld, she ascends
again to the light and is received with rejoicing: new fertility can
begin.[12]

The time of transition, the time of darkness, is full of fear
and terror. Here, at the time of the dark moon, Hecate, another
aspect of the Moon, of "moon nature," works.

Hecate

Hecate is the goddess of the dark moon, of darkness, and of
night. As the daughter of Asteria (the "astral") and Perseus, she
belongs among the oldest gods. Even before Zeus, she was mistress "on Earth and in Heaven and in the Sea," and Zeus "gave
her gifts that were glorious" when he divided the realms
(*Theogony* 412).

Later Hecate could be found everywhere and yet was
nowhere entirely "at home." She is most readily found in dark
places, at thresholds to dark worlds. She is called "Goddess of the
Three Paths" because she knows three worlds. Sacrifices for her
were left at forks in the road ("three roads"), and funeral feasts
were also laid there for restless spirits who she was supposed to
help. She approached at night, announced by howling dogs. She
became the goddess of magic and ghosts, patron of witches. She
can summon evil spirits but also banish them. Hecate conducts
people across thresholds and through transitions. She squats at
the entrance to the depths. She hears Persephone cry out when
Hades abducts her and is one of the first to greet her on her return.

Hecate can promote as well as hinder, as it pleases her
(*Theogony* 429ff). She can cause herds to multiply "at her own
pleasure"; then "she weightens to many out of few, or makes few
out of many" (*Theogony* 446–447). She is invoked at times of difficult births, for she is "the high goddess."

Stelas were erected in front of houses for Hecate so that
she would protect the threshold and exorcise evil. One had to
keep her propitiously disposed, for her proximity was uncanny;
wherever she appeared, the dark was close by.

Hecate's behavior is ambivalent. It is not surprising to find
her at the portal to the underworld. She is familiar with the most
varied reaches of caves and the depths and can conjure the "evil

spirits" that lurk on the threshold to the depths and attack those who enter. She watches over rites of passage; she binds evil and delivers the light. She is midwife, and whatever wants to ascend out of the darkness, she helps toward the light.

Hera

Hera was often associated with the fullest appearance of the Moon. The full moon appears as a sign of the abundance of her power: it casts its light far and revealingly illuminates everything that would hide itself.

The Full Moon manifests in a great many forms: at times, it rises glowing red or orange; three to four hours later at the zenith it beams in pale yellow; and it sets a glistening white while in the East Eos, the "rose-fingered dawn," breaks. And depending how the light of the Moon changes, the appearances of things on the Earth also change from ghostly and uncanny to gently shimmering and calm.

Thus we can experience the fullness of the feminine as gently embracing, protective, enclosing, and assuaging, but also as cold and rejecting, deforming and uncanny. And ultimately, the abundance of the great light of the night must pale before the ascending brightness of the new day.

These images show Hera in her various aspects. At one time, she can be Jupiter's consort, "radiant spouse," especially if she happens also to have borrowed Venus's girdle. As the "white-armed" goddess (*Theogony* 314), she is a bright figure, protectress of the home and hearth, of marriage and of marital fidelity. Then again, she is the severe mistress, and eerily her dark glance tenders something hateful: then she can reveal the demon Lamia, Zeus's lover, and drive her to madness so that she slays her own children. Or she can summon up the "grisly-minded Hydra of Lerna" (*Theogony* 313), that Hercules, her little-loved stepson, must battle. And to make his battle more difficult, she sends Cancer, the crab, to sting him in the heel. She shelters the Nemeian Lion, which was "a plague to mankind" (*Theogony* 329), and again Hercules must fight it. But she could be harsh even to her own son, Hephaestus, who she brought forth from herself "without any act of love" because she was "angered and quarreling with her husband" (*Theogony* 928), and she cast him from Olympus because he displeased her.

Ultimately even Hera must see that a new luminescence is displacing her: young goddesses of following generations of "feminine" possibilities arise, who she would ever so much like to banish from her sight.

The feminine principle, in accord with its nature open to growth, can also become callous and turn into its opposite; it can become dark and destructive and set itself against the light until—to speak in the image of the Moon—it has become entirely empty, and dark, and a new beginning has become necessary and possible. When the light is at its darkest, we know that Persephone will soon return.

The Moon Viewed Psychologically

The Moon principle defines an essential part of the human being and human life. It forms and shapes our emotional attitude to the world and to ourselves. It informs our way of taking things in and dealing with what we have taken in. The lunar quality in us is our emotional impressionability out of which arises the necessity of process, that is, the necessity of actualizing what moves us.

Since the Moon principle plays such an essential role in life, and since it represents the exact opposite of the rationally, actively comprehending principle, it eludes conceptual analysis to an especially high degree. It may be most readily circumscribed by images that each of us carries or can discover within.

I have attempted to circumambulate the Moon principle with the help of myths related to it. Seen from the Chinese t'ai chi, it represents the yin side of humankind and is to be viewed together with the feminine principle.

But just as the feminine principle and woman herself are not identical, neither are the feminine principle and the Moon identical, and certainly the Moon and woman must not be equated. It would be equally wrong to equate Moon and mother, although again and again we are reminded of the maternal aspect in connection with the Moon principle. Mother, woman, daughter, and maiden are each only one image for the Moon principle that dwells in every human being.

In the lunar quality we address our emotional starting point, *our readiness to take in impressions and our ability to respond to them.* Here we reveal the nature of our openness to life, our readiness to receive, to answer, to give.

Early childhood stands in special proximity to the lunar quality. It is a mirror for our impressionability and for the openness of our soul. The child is still embedded wholly in accord with the infinite, completely in the abundance of all things, since it is initially still contained in the mother and hence completely protected by her, receiving from her everything that it needs to live.

The small child—like the lunar part of our soul later on—is similar to an open bowl into which everything falls without selection, be it nourishing and life-giving or burdensome and destructive. But this image also shows the emotional vulnerability that is always contained in the readiness to receive and to take in. This psychic disposition belongs not only to childhood. Again and again, we are immersed in it, whenever we encounter intense experiences. We experience it cyclically in the condition of sleep, the state of being again unconscious. In sleep we are handed over, delivered up, open, for example, to all the images that come up in our dreams. Dreams, fantasies, intimations, and imaginings belong to the domain of the Moon quality in us.

The experience of not separating from childhood and from the Moon's realm is the experience of mother. Here every human being experiences the actual mother in terms of the inner mother image impressed on our psyche as a primordial image (mirrored, for example, in the position of the Moon in the natal horoscope). The image of mother inherent in the psyche is "verified" by the real mother or is projected onto her.

The Moon quality can reveal itself in wildly varying images of mother: it can be life-giving and life-promoting as a primal ground and source of all abundance. Or it can work at binding, restraining, devouring, or suffocating. The mother can be radiant, but also blinding, overpowering. Bright light casts dark shadows, and a mother who appears ever so magnanimous can still be experienced as hard. Her plenitude can also oppress. The image of mother can be unsettling if she is not tangible and present for us, if we experience her as always at a distance and she feels uncontained. Then what she conveys is not containedness and safety but, at best, a bow and arrows, weapons for self-preservation. (If not already apparent, it should now be clear that I am following the in the footsteps of the mythical images as I sketch the variants of the mother image.)

There still remains the image of the witch, who may indeed present herself as helpful (or who behaves helpfully, as does Hecate in the case of Persephone), but in whose realm one must be alert. Here is where one crosses the threshold at which she stands and enters into one's own, new life.

If we attempt to summarize the shadings of Moon qualities found in the various images of the "feminine," the palette includes giving and taking (Selene and Endymion); cherishing and holding fast (Demeter); yearning for, instinctively hitting the mark (Artemis); playfully enjoying, trusting, expecting (Kore); letting oneself sink down, descend, enter (Persephone); holding spellbound, bewitched (Hecate); having radiant vital energy and destroying life (Hera).

The individual qualities, taken by themselves, combine with the other images from one's own experience, and this corresponds to the essence of the Moon quality to weave onward, not to cling to details but to unite everything.

The various aspects of the feminine principle do not represent stages; they are not like steps or a developmental sequence, and most certainly not a scale of values. Rather, they are aspects that again and again resonate anew, psychic modes of experiencing and behaving known to all persons.

Of course, we reencounter many of these aspects in our own actual mother, in mother figures, or in other representatives of the feminine principle. Consciously coming to terms with the the mother imago and with the feminine in general is important for a woman so that she discovers her own *identity as woman.* In this search, the personal mother imago will have profound effects, in both positive and negative senses.

The man experiences the first facets of the feminine principle in the image of the mother and acquires a corresponding attitude to *his particular feminine component, the anima* (in the Jungian sense of the word). He will be influenced and guided in his choice of women and a wife in a way corresponding to this emotional image, again in both positive and negative senses. But, disregarding all human contact, the relationship to the moon quality in him also determines the way he consorts with his own "feminine" values: emotional receptivity as well as his responsive feel.

The effect that the mother imago had in childhood, how the lunar quality presented itself to us, determines our attitude to life in general. If our mother was generous and nurturing, we will always believe that there are positive, life-promoting possibilities. If she appeared rejecting, we will always expect rejection and denial in life and never dare openly request or vulnerably accept.

How we deal with the child in us also corresponds to our lunar disposition: some can accept and be well disposed toward themselves; others view themselves overcritically or anxiously, overtax themselves and are never satisfied.

The Artemis aspect of the lunar quality urges our sensibilities into the open, into *freedom and openness* toward everything natural. With Artemis, we can forsake the parental home and security and learn to defend ourselves and prevail. We need her way

of being in every phase of new advancement and further exploration, whenever we need to slough off old fetters and attain to new inner freedoms.

To the feminine principle also belongs growth and maturation. Devotion belongs to the lunar quality, be it that we let ourselves be swept away, make a sacrifice, or accept the depths in us and in others and let ourselves go. Or it may be a question of surrendering to nature, to all natural life, to all that calls for cherishing and caring.

Equally, the Moon principle signifies having or yearning for abundance. But as the Moon in us indicates, this can come to pass only in change and movement. Part of attainment of abundance is also the necessity of letting go and the strength to go through the dark. Following the Moon principle means accepting the processes of growth that one cannot willfully guide and direct but that one can follow attentively.

The Moon
Book of Planets,
1528

Just as on Earth the oceans flow and ebb through the Moon's power of attraction, so likewise in the psychic realm the moods or the hues of our feeling states rise and fall. Sometimes we are burdened and oppressed by what approaches us, by what is laden upon us, by what falls into our open bowl, and we must work it through. Other times we experience requests and demands as challenges and stimulation.

We experience the cyclical ebb and flow of psychic energy in phases, but also as a daily return: liveliness and vigor, usually in the morning, tiredness, exhaustion, and longing for sleep. This mirrors a general psychic law of energy: to be able to surge ahead, grow, and unfold, there is also need of resting, letting go, letting oneself sink in order then to arise anew. Progression is possible only if, in between, we allow regression (a withdrawal, in sleep, for example).

The myth of Persephone illustrates this: one-third of the year she lives in the underworld in order to bring about fertility two-thirds of the year on the Earth.

The place and time of the myth is here and now. Every month we can experience what the myth grasps in images. Every one of us, man and woman, participates in this, each in his or her own way.

The Moon Viewed Astrologically

It is only to be expected that the astrological and the psychological expositions of the Moon functions would show close resemblances, for the symbol is clearly visible to each of us in its sensorially perceptible form and in its effects, even if strings of symbolic associations to mythological figures did not flourish about it.

In compiling what has been formulated astrologically about the Moon, I summarize by repeating the qualities of psychic receptivity and impressionability, the ability to react to impressions and to stimuli. The Moon is related to childhood and to the impressions experienced in childhood. In childhood, the Moon represents the mother—or the mother figure—who shaped the individual. But the experience of the mother is, to a certain extent, independent of the actual mother, for the child must live in accordance with its own structure, its natal horoscope. This means that the child constellates the mother to a certain extent and effects certain reactions in the mother, just as the child reacts to the mother, responds to her essence, and is influenced by her. (Hence, not all negative memories go back to "objectively" bad mothers! And often there are happier childhood memories than would be expected "objectively.")

Also associated with the Moon are instinct, growth, change; childhood, childlikeness, youthfulness; the unconscious, dream, fantasy, the world of images; openness, changeability of mood, vulnerability; the capacity to receive and to let go; naturalness, rhythmic vitality, soulfulness; tradition, family sense, permanence in change.

As we see, we continue to move ever and again in similar chains of associations, but only in new "translations" of the Moon symbol.

Moon Dreams

In closing, four short dreams that, I believe, are strongly influenced by the lunar quality follow. First, a dream in which Kore transforms into Persephone:

> *I am sitting on a bench in a graveyard. It is night. A bird flies over me; I hear the rustling of its wings. I look up: it is a white dove. She has let something drop into my lap. It is a moonstone. I see how the Moon's light shimmers in it.*

Here is Pluto's proximity—the land of the dead, darkness—and the lure of the rustling wings: "Depart!" A seed of the lunar quality, the yin soul, is dropped into her lap so that it may germinate and bear fruit by day, on Earth. The dream, dreamt long ago, was not forgotten; it needed the time that all growing needs, to "understand" it, that is, to live it.

Another dream, dreamt after the birth of my third child:

> *I am walking on a sunny path toward a great stone doorway. It is very narrow for its size. From the other side, as though from "nowhere," an enormous woman approaches me. I am standing almost in front of her, holding my three children by the hand. Then I see, between us in the middle of the path, that four hyacinths have grown up out of the hard earth.*

Here the hyacinths are not standing in the lush green of the meadow, as in the story of Kore; rather, they have moved into the center, the middle of the path to the portal through which one "crosses over" and whence comes the figure, the goddess from "nowhere." If I were to give this picture a name, it would be "Shy Full Moon": it is not possible to believe that the full moon—almost—has really been reached. The four strongly fragrant hyacinths in full bloom form the midpoint, the central concern. They are an image of the union of above and below: they sprout from the bulbs in the dark Earth, break through the hard crust of the path, and blossom in the light. And there are four of them, the number of totality, wholeness.

I am holding the children by the hand, full of future, and in the figure of the great woman the high point and the beginning of the end steps through the portal. She reminds me of Dore Hoyer, an exponent of German expressive dance, who had just retired from public performance at the time. This was an encounter at the pinnacle, in broad daylight, and the way through to the other side, the beginning descent, a possible image for the full moon.

Two additional dream images speak for themselves.

> *Renate (that was really her name, the "one reborn," a long-deceased childhood friend) hands me a photo from our youth. It is a group picture with the two of us in the middle. Attached to the reverse is a piece of tissue paper on which is written all the names in order. I look at the photograph more closely and see that, although it was taken probably more than thirty years ago, we already looked then like we do today. But then I look even more closely. Were those girls perhaps our mothers who looked so much like us?*

And the second dream:

> *In my hand I am holding a page from an album and with difficulty recognize that I had written it. I must have written it many years ago. Is it a poem? A page from a diary? As I read it, I find the very tiny signature, "Ida," and recognize that it is a page from my grandmother.*

Seamless transition between the generations, the ages run together. Moon time knows no linear course, no historical beginning, no set end. What my grandmother wrote could be mine; what we are or were, our mothers could have been. The Moon is the wheel of growing, maturing, passing away, and beginning anew. Mythic time weaves in the Moon principle: always, and always now.

The Sun

The sign of the Sun forms the counterpart to the lunar, "feminine," or yin principle. Whereas softness, water, attraction, receiving, and taking is lunar, fire, strength, and moving and effective force is solar. Here the "masculine" or yang principle counters the feminine or yin principle. The polarity of the two principles is clearly evident: day and night, light and darkness, strength and weakness, masculine and feminine, doing and receiving.

Tension, movement, and life itself arise from the fundamental antithesis of Sun and Moon, solar and lunar, yang and yin, for life is not possible without movement. Life is an energetic process and has need of polarities so that a gradient and play of energy can arise. "The tension of opposites that makes energy possible is a universal law, fittingly expressed in the yang and the yin of Chinese philosophy" (Jung 1948, par. 291).

Sun and Moon, Ch'ien and K'un, yang and yin, masculine and feminine principles are perfect counterparts that do not combat but rather complement, that mutually promote and limit each other: the one cannot exist without the other. Light exists only because of the dark; day is unthinkable without night. The creative needs the receptive in which it can work and come to realization. Here, we clearly sense that by the feminine principle of the Moon and the masculine principle of the Sun we do not mean personal qualities that are assigned to those who play the role of man or woman. Rather, it is a question of two principles, inherent in human beings, that mutually depend on and reciprocally influence each other.

The Myth of Helios

Among the Greeks at the time of Hesiod and Homer, the Sun, Helios, was not a god who intervened in human life and who one encountered in cult. Nor had Jupiter accorded him a specific domain in the world or in life; rather, he was the supreme ruler of the light and himself always in motion. Helios was revered as an immediate natural phenomenon, as the symbol of ascent and descent, life, light, and order. Morning and evening, one greeted Helios the Sun when it rose or set.

In the myth, it is told that Helios had one palace in the east and one in the west. Every morning, he left the palace in the east with his four horses, drove through the high arch of heaven, and in the evening descended again to his western palace. Then he sailed in a vessel through the depths of the ocean back to the palace of the east, only to rise again in the morning. Later, it was told that he and his team embarked from the west in a golden boat that Hephaestus had made for him and then slept.

The major qualities of Helios were his team of horses and his ability to see everything. Thus, it came about that he revealed to Hephaestus the love affair of Aphrodite and Ares. But he also knew what transpired in the darkness of the underworld and thus knew of Persephone's fate. But Helios was not always attentive. Thus, for example, he did not notice how his companions stole Odysseus's cattle.

The Sun and His Children
Woodcut by Hans Sebald Beham, ca. 1530

The most varied forms of energy become images in the myth of Helios.

Energy as *power* is revealed in the four horses that draw his sun chariot. Still today, we express our locomotion in terms of horsepower. Helios also reveals energy as *movement*. Solar energy can move or propel not only the sun chariot but also the modern automobile. Helios radiates energy as *light* and *warmth* and at night embodies *potential energy* (resting in the vessel, he regenerates his strength).

Here kinetic, radiant, and potential energy are expressed in impressive pictures, and it also becomes clear how one form of energy can be transformed into another, a physical law that is as true in modern physics as in the ancient mythological formulation.

The Sun Viewed Psychologically

In the symbol of the Sun, the soul finds a reflection of the entire energy potential available to human beings: vital energy, living impulses, all possible intensity of life.

In human life there are also various forms of energy, and one can be transformed into another or one can bring about the other. Thanks to the power and strength of our muscles, we can move; movement causes us to feel warm, and we radiate warmth; we must regenerate ourselves in the state of rest. All this holds true in the physical as it does, analogously, in the psychic domain.

In Jungian terminology, this vital energy is called *libido* and embraces all the energy available to human beings, physical and psychic. Through experience—even if we are not always conscious of it—we are very well aware that one form of energy can be transformed into any other.

A strong heart lets us run fast, be cordial toward persons, or approach a task or theme with intensity; we warm to an idea, our hearts beat faster when we are moved, and so on.

Strength, moving and being moved; radiance, warmth, clarity of consciousness; rest, recuperation, collecting our forces; all are experiences in psychic as in physical life and can also be seen in connection with our libido as forms of kinetic, radiant, or potential energy.

In the image of the four-horse team, the Sun corresponds to the vital energy that sets things in motion, brings about activity, and signifies creative power.

As a psychic phenomenon, the Sun presupposes the center of the personality or ego center; the consciousness of one's own identity: I am I. Only this ego consciousness makes possible consciousness of, and reflection on, what has been experienced. Various features, all contained in the symbol of the sun, belong to ego consciousness: the ego knows itself as an actively creative force. It experiences itself as a totality that indeed senses the tension of various pairs of opposites in itself, that can be exposed to conflicts, but that, as a whole person, is always an "I," an ego. Its whole life long, the ego remains identical with itself: from childhood into old age the ego, despite all the changes in our bodies and in our souls, remains the same ego, the same kernel of the personality. The "I" or ego experiences itself as something self-evident and unique with its own power, its own intentions, its own will (i.e., with consciously disposable psychic energy).

The ego consciousness must not be confused with the intellect (which, among the planetary symbols, is assigned not to the Sun but to Mercury). This center or kernel of the personality (which is indicated in the natal horoscope with the glyph of the Sun) does not represent the totality of the individual but rather offers a precondition for the possibility of wholeness, for "seeing" and living the other psychic functions or parts of the personality. (With regard to the path of individuation postulated by Jung, this would be only the path from the "I" or ego of the Sun to the Self of wholeness.)[13]

In the sign of the Sun we find the seam between body and soul, physical and psychic energy, as well as between consciousness and the unconscious.

With the myth of Helios I have, up to this point, traced only the upper arc of power and movement and of the light. There yet remains the night sea journey, Helios's return voyage in the vessel through the depths of the ocean that flows about the entire world.

Here we see the same psychic law of energy that we met when we considered the Moon cycles: progression, ascent, brightness, light, and power lead to an countermovement, a transformation of the energy: in the regression—the return path through the darkness—passivity reigns. Helios lies sleeping in the vessel or the ferry; he lets the stream of the ocean carry him, and new energy accumulates that will again be transformed in the morning into activity when the Sun begins to arise in the east.

While mastery of the day corresponds to the activity of ego consciousness, during the night it is "laid to rest." In sleep there is no longer a conscious "I," but rather only unconsciousness or a dream ego (the "I" that acts and experiences in the dream) which must again be rejoined to the conscious ego or "I" upon awakening; this succeeds if and when dreams are recalled and integrated into consciousness. But here we need the help of Mercury, the mediator between above and below, consciousness and the unconscious.

Just like Helios in the myth, we discover that we do not perceive or see much even with clear daytime consciousness, because such consciousness shuns our attention. On the other hand, with a bit of effort and application, we can raise all sorts of things up out of the darkness of the underworld, out of the unconscious, into the light of day, into consciousness.

Just as the Sun sets the rhythm of day and night, our inner Sun determines our energy potential and the play of forces in both the physical and the psychic realms, from day to day and from one stage of life to another; and it determines how we turn toward specific areas of life as well as the way we see and experience the world.

The Sun Viewed Astrologically

Again it is obvious, as was the case in our astrological commentary on the Moon symbol, that astrological and psychological points of view coincide to a great degree, since we can experience the bearer of the projections of our inner essence of the Sun both as a symbol and as energy working on us from outside equally visible to and experienced by all.

I will mention a number of associations that, to some extent, repeat what we have already said. The Sun can be seen as center of the personality, the ego; as vital will, force, or strength; as ego strength, but also as egotism; as self-worth, self-affirmation, self-assurance; but also as desire to dominate, as power drive; the Sun signifies the center of power, source of energy, readiness to act, activity; boldness, courage, influence, charisma, authority; will, perseverance; etc.

We see that we are circumambulating a specific kernel and encountering very different gradations of meaning. And with this we have left behind the general consideration of the Sun symbol.

If we want a closer approximation to the various aspects of the Sun, we must consider the signs of the zodiac.

II

The Zodiac

The Zodiac Man
(late thirteenth century)

The Zodiac, the Sun, and Precession

Before we consider the twelve signs of the zodiac, which express the various qualities of the Sun, we must address certain fundamental thoughts: the fact that, as earth dweller, humankind experiences itself as dependent on the Sun, the Sun's light, and on the seasons as determined by the Sun's position, and has attempted, since time immemorial, to discern the interconnections between the Sun's position and the celestial bodies that surround us. In addition, we must briefly look into what is called precession, an astronomical phenomenon which, on the one hand, plays a role in criticisms of astrology and, on the other hand, is related to the often mentioned astrological ages ("Age of Aquarius," etc.). Moreover, we must clarify the difference between the *astronomical constellation* and the *sign of the zodiac*.

Just as the Earth relates to the Sun and is regulated by the Sun's force field, and just as all growth on Earth is dependent on the Sun's light, so too is humankind. Biologically, sociologically, and also psychologically, humankind depends on the Sun: on the alternation of light and dark; on the rhythms of the seasons, and the associated energy force fields.

How different the feeling for life is in the summer, when

87

the Sun has reached its zenith and beams the hottest, when the abundant fruits begin to ripen and bright flowers blossom, than in the winter when the Sun rises for only a few hours and its light falls obliquely, pale and giving little warmth, when all growth seems interrupted and nature brings forth no radiant colors.[14] It is not surprising that animals as different as the lion and the ibex arise as images symbolizing these differing qualities of light and warmth: the lion, living in hot regions, the "king of animals," as the powerful and strong sign of summer, and the undemanding ibex, adapted to a raw environment, as the image of winter.

All people are influenced by the changes of light, the alternation of the seasons of the year; but not all react in the same way to these changes. We call ourselves day or night, morning or evening persons because at certain times we feel fresher and better than at others. We do not all feel best during the hot summer months; every body responds to the qualities of the Sun's warmth in its own way. This does not happen by chance or arbitrarily but in harmony with the individual's inner psychic structure or natal chart, and hence with the "inner" Sun of which we spoke in the preceding chapter. The vital energy (that appears in the Sun sign in the natal horoscope and with which each person is uniquely endowed) and the energies thus available stipulate very different ways of experiencing the world.

Just as we cannot perceive the world around us without the Sun's light, we cannot—psychologically speaking—realize any perception if it is not reflected in consciousness. To this extent, an analogy exists between the actual Sun and the consciousness symbolized by the Sun. Likewise there is a parallel between the light and warmth conditions (or the energy fields) of the outer world and the "inner" Sun as symbol for the physical and psychic energy of the individual.

Besides observing the movements of the Sun, human attention has been drawn since time immemorial to the moving starry sky. Daily it completes a rotation about a fixed pole from east to west (if we look from north to south). In the northern hemisphere, this is approximately the pole star, which is less than one degree distant from the north pole and easy to find. The surrounding stars move concentrically about it. On the other hand, we see in the proximity of the eastern horizon new constellations continually arising, which then descend in the west. Each night, rising and setting shift by a few seconds, and the constellations can be seen in the same positions again only after a whole year passes. Hence, to the human eye they appear to move like the Sun and return to the same place.[15]

Early astronomers recognized that by observing the fixed stars they could also establish the position of the Sun more precisely. For the sake of better orientation, the vault of the heavens was divided into various constellations, into groupings of bright fixed stars that could be easily recognized at any time; they saw certain figures in these groupings, to which they gave certain names. At the beginning of the Christian era, forty-eight constellations had been recognized and cataloged. Today the entire sky is divided into eighty-eight different, large, but precisely delimited constellation areas.

In the catalog of stars compiled by Hipparchus (circa 190–125 B.C.E.), more than one thousand stars are listed by name.[16] Already some two thousand years before Copernicus, Aristarchus of Samos (circa 310–250 B.C.E.) developed a heliocentric system. And 150 years B.C.E., Hipparchus had discovered the precession of Earth's axis, the significance of which is only today being measured.

The twelve known constellations belong among the oldest signs of the zodiac. They were of special significance because they form the background for the movements of the Sun, the Moon, and the planets, the background of the apparent course of the Sun. This path, which in actuality is the orbit of Earth about the Sun, is called the ecliptic.[17] In the course of the year, the Sun, from our point of view, traverses the plane of the ecliptic, and each month one of the twelve constellations forms the background for this section of the path. Since seven of the twelve constellations are animal figures, they were collectively called the *zodiac* (from the Greek *zoon*, "animal," plus *kylos*, "circle").

The constellations are of varying sizes, and the Sun takes differing lengths of time to traverse each. Thus it is only in Cancer (the crab) for nineteen days but can be seen for forty-three days in the constellation Virgo (the virgin).[18] For the sake of a more simply calculated calendar, the twelve sectors of the ecliptic were divided into equal-sized sections of thirty degrees each and then named for the corresponding constellations. This made sense because people were not concerned with the observation and investigation of the constellations but rather with describing the path of the Sun that is so very decisive and formative for life on Earth. The background constellations serve only an orienting function.

Here we must clearly differentiate the zodiacal *constellation* from the zodiacal *sign*. The constellation in the zodiac is an astronomically determined constellation area in the vault of the heavens of varying magnitude, which includes a specific number of fixed stars. The sign of the zodiac does indeed bear the name of the constellation (which serves for orientation), but it designates a specific sector of the Sun's path, the ecliptic, of fixed size (thirty degrees) and thus also designates certain qualities of the Sun that we on Earth can distinctly recognize.

For us, certain Sun qualities are intimately associated with the signs of the zodiac. For this reason, the signs of the zodiac became carriers of projections of important human experiences over the course of time. In them, we experience the rhythm of energy in the course of the year.

The fact that all planets except Pluto move within the plane of the ecliptic elevates it to a special level of importance. Various correspondences and relationships were—and still are today—experienced among the qualities of the planets as expressed in myths and the energy structures reflected in the twelve signs of the zodiac. We can perhaps better understand that these experiences have nothing to do with the fixed stars if we call to mind certain orders of magnitude and the astronomical numbers. To the naked eye, the planets appear larger and more luminous than most fixed stars, although we also see some fixed stars that approximate the size of the planets or shine even more brightly. But the differences between the planets and the fixed stars is very great when expressed numerically.

The light that the planets reflect reaches us in a few hours, even from Uranus, Neptune, and Pluto, the most distant planets. By contrast, the light of the fixed stars takes years to get to Earth, a light-year being equal to approximately six trillion miles. The fixed star Pollux in Gemini is "only" thirty-two light-years away from us, and shining Regulus in Leo eighty-five light-years (but because it is 400 times as bright as the Sun, it can be seen easily as it brightly shines). The light of Spica in Virgo takes 260 years to arrive; that of Antares in Scorpio takes nearly twice as long, 500 years till it reaches us (a distance of 500 times six trillion miles). Moreover, the fixed star Antares is 700 times larger than our Sun and 80,000 times brighter. Thus it appears as large as a planet to the naked eye, but the light that reaches us was emitted 500 years ago.[19]

Life on Earth is determined by the Sun, as are the courses of the planets. However, the various qualities of the Sun are expressed—in the calendar as well as astrologically—by the Sun's position in the ecliptic, the belt of the zodiac.

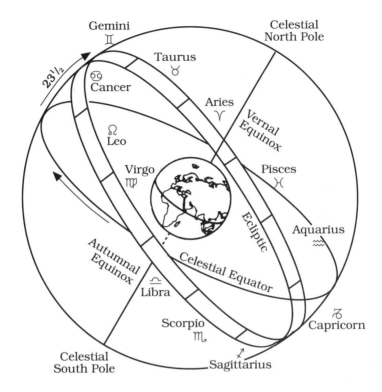

The Celestial Equator and the Ecliptic

The belt of the zodiac lies at an angle to the celestial equator (which can be imagined as an infinite extension of the Earth's equator). The angle between zodiac and equator equals 23.5° and is called the inclination of the plane of the ecliptic. The celestial equator is perpendicular to the celestial axis, the extended Earth axis.

At the time of the equinoxes, the Sun passes the intersection of the zodiac and the celestial equator, i.e., on March 21 at 0° Aries (the first day of spring) moving toward the northern hemisphere and 0° Libra where the descent to the southern hemisphere begins on September 23. Thus, the spring and autumn points always occur at 0° of the zodiacal signs Aries and Libra even if the constellations Aries and Libra no longer form the background for these positions of the Sun.

For example, the expression, "I'm an Aries," means that the speaker was born between March 21 and April 20 when the

Sun passes through that section of the ecliptic identified with the zodiacal sign of Aries.

At the time when the spring and fall equinoxes were positioned on the ecliptic (about 300 B.C.E.), their position actually corresponded to the visual perception of their location. But already 150 years later, Hipparchus noticed a displacement of the point of the vernal equinox, that is, a displacement of the astronomical constellation Aries and the zodiacal sign Aries on the ecliptic. This displacement amounted to one degree in about seventy-two years, a degree corresponding to twice the diameter of the Moon. Since establishing the zodiacal point of the vernal equinox, approximately 2,300 years have passed. According to Hipparchus, this would result in a displacement of some 32 degrees, and this figure is astonishingly close to the most recent calculations. By sight, this means that on March 21 the Sun is still deep in Pisces and reaches the sign Aries only on April 18.

Hipparchus called this displacement "precession," since he assumed that the fixed stars of the ecliptic plane very slowly "advance" or "precede," following the movement of the advancing Sun. Three hundred years later, however, Ptolemy determined that the positions of the constellations in the ecliptic and elsewhere remained the same. Within the celestial sphere there is no change of position among the stars except in relation to the Sun's path. Since the time of Copernicus, we have known that the daily rotations of the stars and the annual cycle of the Sun are only apparent movements that actually come about through two movements of the Earth: the daily rotation of the Earth on its axis and the Earth's orbit around the Sun.

Modern physics has been able to explain the precession also as a movement of the Earth. The Earth's axis, which is positioned at an angle to the orbital plane, describes a cone as turns, hence it does not remain fixed in relation to its midpoint. Thus, the celestial axis (the extension of the Earth's axis) no longer aligns precisely with the pole star; rather, as a consequence of the precession, the celestial north pole describes a retrograde circle through the constellations near the north pole. In the course of 25,800 years, the stars located on this circle become the pole star, one after another.

As the north pole and the pole star shift, so too the point of the spring equinox moves backward over the millennia, taking 25,800 years to return to its original position of 0° Aries.

Our solar year, the so-called tropical year (*tropos*, in Greek, means "turning," referring here to the two "turns" of the

Sun, the solstices) which determines the rhythm of the seasons, is somewhat shorter than the so-called sidereal year (*sider* means "stars"), which is calculated on the basis of the Sun's return to a position in relation to a given fixed star. The differential is very small, 20.5 minutes per year. But in 25,800 years, this amounts to one full year, which is called a *precessional year* or *great year*. During this period of time, the vernal equinox moves backwards to its "original" position at 0° Aries.

These are not merely calculations or abstract reflections. We are confronted by such facts, for example, when we read monthly reports of celestial phenomena, such as those published in newspapers at the end of one month for the coming month. When we read there that Mars is moving through Taurus, we can actually see the planet in that constellation, if the time and the atmospheric conditions are favorable. But if we look in an ephemeris, the tables that indicate the planetary positions in the signs of the zodiac, i.e., in the seasonally determined portion of the ecliptic, we find Mars already "rushing" through the sign Gemini. At the same time, Saturn is astronomically in the morning sky in the constellation Scorpio, but in the tables of the ephemeris, Saturn's position is in the zodiacal sign Sagittarius.

Determining the precession is of great importance in astronomy; for astrology, it is meaningless. Astronomy (Greek for "knowledge of the stars") is the study of stars, of their spatial arrangement, movement, constitution, and of the development of heavenly bodies. It is the oldest science and became one of the most modern by its connections to physics, meteorology, geoscience, technology, etc. Astrology is not a science of the stars in this sense. Astrology is not at all interested in the billions of celestial bodies, not even in the celestial vault itself. Of significance here are only the "moving stars," the planets, which change in space in relationship to the Earth, the Sun, and in their positions to each other. Where astronomy turns its gaze outward into the infinite, which humankind continually seeks and continues to measure, astrology turns its gaze, so to speak, inward, from the image of the external world to the inner structure of the human being. The astonishing thing is that in the human microcosm we find analogies to the macrocosm of the universe, as the modern natural sciences reveal.

In astrological observation, we are concerned with the oldest questions of humanity, ever and again posed by the awakening consciousness of the individual and taken up by religion and philosophy: Where do I come from? Who am I? What is my goal?

For questions of this sort, precession is without meaning. What remain are the planets, the representatives of numinous experiences or archetypal structures. There remain also the signs of the zodiac, determined by the Sun, as deposits of the experience of certain rhythms in the physical as in the psychic life. And, in addition, there is finally the reference to the individual person, to the place and hour of his or her birth, and thus to the individual possibilities of life as they are understood in the system of the houses of the zodiac.

The Signs of the Zodiac

The twelve signs of the zodiac can be regarded as twelve facets of the Sun symbol. These signs are, first of all, not symbols in the sense defined at the beginning of this book. Likewise, the individual fixed stars that comprise the constellations of the zodiac are not symbols as are, for example, the planets. The constellations—and especially those of the zodiac—do not lend themselves to forming a sensuously perceptible Gestalt that could appear suited as a vehicle for a symbol. Granted, people have attempted to sketch fantastic, expressive figures in the astrological star map; but individual stars contributing to the images are difficult to find in those figures and sometimes appear at insignificant positions within.

What was comprehended in the signs of the zodiac can be understood only through the formative experiences of the various Sun qualities for which they became the symbolic carriers, not through observation of the fixed stars to which they belong.

So for the constellations of the zodiac, there are actually few impressive or independent myths and legends, whereas for other constellations we can find numerous legends from the world of Greek heroes (Schadewaldt 1956).

The glyphs that usually designate the signs of the zodiac correspond to a hieroglyphic in which an intended content is sketched graphically in a concise form.

♈ ♉ ♊ ♋ ♌ ♍ ♎ ♏ ♐ ♑ ♒ ♓

Nevertheless, since time immemorial, the signs of the zodiac—in all astrological traditions—have been experienced as true symbols. People believed they sensed some effective energy in them and saw in them a likeness of supraordinate principles they could intuit, or actually establish, as was the case with the planets or planetary gods. And from the features of the signs of the zodiac, inferences were drawn concerning those born under them.

From the viewpoint of contemporary psychology, we could say that since the earliest times human beings have seen and experienced in the outer world what is already inherent in their own structure. In relation to the zodiac, this is especially obvious, for the human being, as an earthling, is absolutely subject to the events and conditions on Earth. And these, in turn, are subject to the position of the Sun in relation to Earth. We are born into very specific, terrestrial conditions and are informed by them. And we cannot experience or consciously perceive the world about us, no matter how distant, other than in projections that correspond to our inner structures.

The human soul has elevated the celestial background of that which shapes and informs us to the level of a symbol. In this sense, we can say that the twelve signs of the zodiac are different facets of the symbol of the Sun. When we do this, we must once again remember that we do not voluntarily make projections; rather, they happen to us. They reach out into the universe and confront us with what lies closest by: our inner structure, or our own soul. First we must experience abundance or stinginess, softness or hardness, fire or water "out there," in the external world, before we can see the correspondences in our physical or psychic life; until, in fact, we finally even consider it possible that we can, or must, have our experiences in the outer world only because of our inner structure.

By adducing the myths of the gods in considering the planets for whom they were named, we discovered analogies to the psychic functions in us. We saw them as form-giving primordial patterns, as archetypes of our soul.

In considering the signs of the zodiac that relate to the Sun's qualities and the seasonal rhythms, we encounter analogies between the conditionality of organic life on Earth and our own physical conditionality. But here we cannot make an absolute distinction between physical and psychic functions. They condition each other. Only with the help of the functions of our soul are we able to perceive the physical functions at all.

It is logical that in astrology every sign of the zodiac is assigned a planet that is particularly suited to express the psychic component of the given physical qualities of the zodiacal sign. Indeed, the sign of the zodiac often becomes "comprehensible" only thanks to the planet.

In astrological interpretation, it is a question of concurrently seeing the symbolic images of the zodiacal sign and the psychic tendencies recognizable in it, brought together in the planet. If physical and psychic structures first were projected into the external world and into the symbolic image, the zodiacal sign, now the path leads back into the psyche and the physical constitution of the individual human being. The projection is withdrawn when we recognize external facts as inner structures, when we see external limitation as inner constitution and possibility.

This sounds almost mystical. But Paracelsus (as physician) and Kepler (as astronomer) both spoke of an "inner zodiac," by which they meant a structure peculiar to the psyche that represents not "only" an analogy to the "external" zodiac but rather one that, in fact, participates in the cosmic order or reveals a correspondence to the external zodiac (Strauss-Kloebe 1984, p. 84).

All persons participate in all twelve signs of the zodiac, for we are—from our point of view—surrounded by the zodiac. In each natal chart or horoscope, the circle of the twelve signs of the zodiac forms the basic pattern, the background, for one's individual existence. Depending on the year, day, and hour of birth, the planets are variously distributed across the zodiac.

The ten planets were assigned to the twelve signs of the zodiac in such a way that the Sun and the Moon belong to only one sign each that fully corresponds to their natures; the first five planets were assigned to two signs each, one active and one passive, a form corresponding to yang and yin.

The diagram below shows the assignment of the planets discovered later—Uranus, Neptune, and Pluto. That a correspondence of planet and sign actually does exist will become evident when we consider the corresponding sign of the zodiac.

Now we surrender the symmetry to a dynamic that we will trace in the following discussion.

When I consider the signs of the zodiac, I will briefly refer each time to the position of the Sun, that is, the seasonal light conditions; then I will turn to the symbolic image. I will then re-

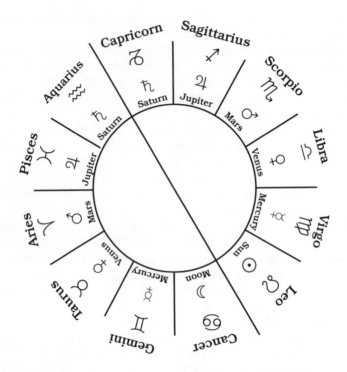

late both to the planet assigned to them, for only the assigned planet permits recognition of the psychic aspect which the zodiacal sign can represent. As was the case when we considered the planetary symbolism, so here positive and negative aspects—light and shadowy sides—appear, in keeping with the conscious or unconscious attitude toward the qualities manifested in the sign. Finally, I will refer to the bodily region to which each of the twelve zodiacal signs was assigned in older astrology, in order again to refer to the organically reflected or "material" side of the zodiacal sign.

Previously, astrologers derived far-reaching pronouncements regarding body structure, physiognomy, and predisposition to illnesses from the zodiacal signs. I can only allude to this theme, but I would not want to omit mentioning the physical aspect entirely (see Reimann 1977; Adler 1950). These assumptions of the older astrological tradition cannot, of course, be supported in any manner by contemporary medical and physiological thought. Nevertheless, the presence of such correspondences in

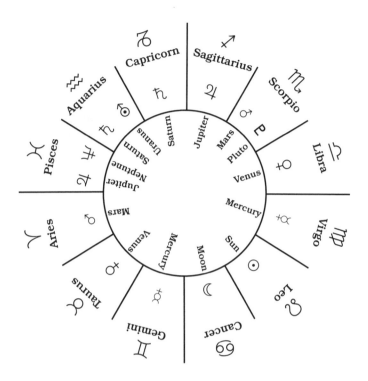

the sense of a body language seems to me plausible, and in many cases it can be observed.

In interpreting the signs of the zodiac, I will utilize various sources and points of view, since here we cannot rely on comprehensive and contemporaneous sources such as Hesiod and Homer (as we did when discussing the planetary gods). For one thing, the signs of the zodiac are especially old and were already well known throughout the entire Mediterranean area when they played a relatively insignificant role for the Greeks; for another, complete presentations of the material, as far as I know, are lacking.

I am not striving for the most comprehensive depiction of the signs of the zodiac possible. They cannot be interpreted exhaustively. They have become too thoroughly symbols for that. It is the essence of the symbol that it points to a power transcending itself, one that we circumambulate but can never grasp.

This is also not the place to elaborate what it means when

a planet is not in its "own" sign, to which it is suited by its essence, but rather in another sign that perhaps is diametrically opposed to its essence, nor to discuss how we are to understand a cluster of several planets in the same sign. I do hope to be able to impart enough information that the reader's courage and desire to further consider astrology awakens.

It is unavoidable that, from time to time, I will use the name of a sign of the zodiac in a personified way, speaking of "an Aries," or "a Taurus," or "a Gemini," when I refer to a person who is informed by the qualities of that sign of the zodiac.

Aries

Planet Mars
March 21—April 21

The zodiacal sign Aries begins on March 21 when the Sun crosses the celestial equator toward the north. That is the time of the vernal equinox. In the northern hemisphere, light increasingly predominates from now on. spring has begun, and the year "increases," that is, light and growth increase.

We sense and experience the conclusive victory of light, the waxing power of the Sun, a real "new" year. The frozen Earth awakens, tender shoots push through and seem especially bright following the colorless season before. Everything announces awakening and new life. Hence Aries—imagined as leaping—is also the symbol of life arising anew. The senses open to the new beginnings: it "smells" like spring. The feeling of increasing energy and vitality awakens in most people.

The equinoxes and the solstices are the most noteworthy points in the Sun's orbit: balance between light and dark; increase of the light to the zenith; decrease to the shortest day when, following the Winter solstice, the Sun begins again to ascend and the days grow longer.[20] These four prominent positions marking Spring, Summer, Fall, and Winter are called cardinal points. The zodiacal signs associated with them—Aries, Cancer, Libra, and Capricorn—are cardinal signs. Each stands at the beginning of a new season and marks the beginning of a new quadrant. They have been observed and ritually celebrated in almost all cultures up until modern times. The second sign in each quadrant has traditionally been designated as "fixed" and the third as "mutable." Moreover, each zodiacal sign is assigned an element: fire, earth, air, or water (Ring 1956-1973). (I will return to the significance of these attributes in greater detail in the last chapter.)

Aries

The symbolic animal of the beginning of spring is Aries, the ram. Only wild sheep reveal their true essence; tamed and domesticated, their uniqueness turns into its opposite. Wild sheep are full of life, quick, agile, nimble. We are often familiar only with the lethargic, expressionless, dull domestic animals that certainly are not referred to in the zodiacal sign.

The ram—like all wild sheep—lives in mountainous areas and loves the heights. With the waxing light and the ascending season, he migrates from the low lands to the highest heights, even above the snow line; when winter comes, he again descends. Rams climb agilely and daringly; they have a "lively spirit," display "clever understanding," and avoid danger (Brehm 1876–1878. vol. 4).[21] But if they encounter rivals, or if they are otherwise challenged, their pugnacity awakens. Rams fight to a definitive end: victory or defeat. That can happen in an instant. Approach and attack follow impulse, and when the obstacle has been vanquished or overcome, "pure joi de vivre" or the urge to new undertaking rules again.

As skillful as the ram is in jumping and climbing, it displays correspondingly little endurance if it must traverse longer distances. As a leader, the ram can be ruthless. He eliminates his rivals, but when the danger is greater, he flees and leaves the flock and the young in the lurch. These animals are sexually mature at the age of one year; all in all, they are very vital and prolific.

Many of the characteristics of the ram correspond to qualities ascribed to Mars. His turbulent, untamed, volatile nature did not make him beloved of his mother Hera and of the other Olympians. Love of conflict, changeable impulses, destructive rage, inconstancy, and "fickleness" were experienced in him. We might call to mind the tumult and the carnage of the herd that plunges thoughtlessly into battle or unnecessary dangers, blindly following the ram.

Mars ardently approached Venus and begat Fear and Terror but also Eros and Harmonia when he was lovingly accepted. If undirected, his energy was quick to destroy; properly employed, on the other hand, it had great impact and capacity to persevere.

The image of the ram helps express what we can sense in the symbol of this zodiacal sign. And the qualities that are ascribed to the planet Mars and are so similar to the essence of the ram illustrate this most impressively. The animal migrating to the heights as spring begins points to the ascending Sun, to rising vitality, and to new impulses, germinating possibilities.

In ancient Egypt, the image of the ram was found in the same context. There it was the sacred animal of the creator god Chnum who, among other things, created humankind on the potter's wheel. Fertility and new creation were also celebrated at the spring festivals in which a ram served as sacrificial animal. Its intact skeleton was offered to the deity as a guarantee that new life and resurrection are possible.

Likewise in the Old Testament a ram served as sacrificial

animal: Isaac owed the sparing of his life to the ram. The feast of Easter, resurrection from death, takes place in the sign of the ram, Aries, on the first Sunday after the spring new moon.

This sign of the zodiac embraces all the traits of origins and new beginnings: approach and leap, impetus, driving power, love of battle, persistence, the urge to press forward, striving for the heights, to the light. Aries qualities and Mars functions are powers that work formatively at this time: taking by storm, blowing up, thrusting, jumping, piercing, erupting, penetrating, vanquishing, fructifying, destroying, leaping over obstacles, restlessness, urgency, impetus. Corresponding to the fiery nature of Aries and Mars, the element fire was associated with this sign of the zodiac.

Understood psychically, corresponding to the "inner zodiac," these qualities are expressed as activity and initiative; obstinacy, bellicosity, and irritability; restlessness, vehemence, rapidity, thrusting forward; youthful impatience; erotic sexual urge to conquer; lack of empathy, but still the desire to be fully accepted in spite of, indeed with all one's wildness; the wish for balance achieved through loving completion (as in the instance of Mars and Venus). This is not easily attained through ruthlessness, changeable impulses, strong affects, pugnacity, and meager adaptability, nor is it made easy for the other; but there remains a longing, a yearning, that drives one onward. On the other hand, self-will prohibits Aries from accepting subordination. Aries is extraordinarily sensitive vis-à-vis authority, limitation of turf, in the concrete as well as in the psychic realm.

In the body, the sign Aries is associated with the head. "Headstrong" in getting one's way or "losing one's head" and panicking—these are possibilities inherent in the nature of Aries and of Mars, as is falling "head over heels" or passionately in love which can be sudden but may not last.

If we assume that the human being is a unity of psyche and soma, it is not difficult to suppose that negative bodily consequences are possible if the primary, inherent nature of the individual cannot freely develop. This is true for all signs of the zodiac and for the psychic functions contained in them. If one cannot consciously accept one's innate potentials and integrate them into one's life, they turn into disturbances, illnesses, or morbid traits. Usually, it is not only the individual who is responsible for this. Environment, milieu, and societal demands are also involved, even if not apparent from the horoscope. What the natal horoscope does show are the original inclinations and structures; and if one is not successful in living in accord with them, these possibilities turn into their opposite. They are repressed into the shadow, or lead a shadowy existence for a long time, unwanted, forbidden, and unrecognized even in their positive aspect.

Instead of initiative and activity, one experiences aggression, which, if not admitted, turns into passive aggression: one suspects a possible enemy, or something evil, in everyone else, and one encounters the other with a negative expectation that radiates one's own, passive, stance of aggression. It is also possible that the aggression is turned not outward but inward, self-destructively against oneself.

Whoever cannot live his or her own power suffers feelings of anxiety and (actual) impotence. Whoever cannot tackle a problem often grinds his teeth at night. In this context, one can well imagine that headaches, migraines, sleep disturbances, etc., are consequences of unlived Mars/Aries possibilities.

Taurus

Planet Venus
April 22—May 21

The Sun has ascended one more month. The days are noticeably longer and warmer. Colors in nature are thriving. The initially changeable, unreliable "April weather" yields to a more constant warmth. We are reassured: it is spring, summer will come. The green crops have sprouted, and it is time to set out plants.

The segment of the ecliptic that the Sun now traverses is characterized by Taurus, the bull. Again we have a horned, male animal, and yet the bull, Taurus, represents quite different qualities than Aries, the ram. Where Aries loved activity and the heights, Taurus is comfortable in the lowlands, on soft, lush meadows, in contented passivity. The contrasts could scarcely be greater than between the heaven-storming little ram, the animal of the creator god Chnum, and the bull with his feet firmly planted on the ground. He was the sacred animal of the Egyptian earth god, Apis.

In almost all religions the bull has played a significant role, and thanks to his impressively powerful form, he became the symbol of strength and fertility in many places: in India, Persia, Crete, in the cult of Mithras, and among the Celts. He was re-garded as the bearer of fertility, as fructifier of the earth, as the life-giving and life-preserving source, but also as the fertility of the Earth it-self, as the symbolic vehicle of the earth god. In ancient Babylon, he was seen as the fructi-fier and preserver of the life force, as he who delivered the water of life. In Egypt, people ex-perienced the annual flooding of the Nile that irrigated their fields and thus was a vital ne-cessity as the "gift of the bull." Fertility in  general is experienced as an essential quality of the bull symbol, not only in the sense of active fertilization, but above all as fruit-ful growth, as the fertility of the Earth, of the field, in whose fur-rows—ploughed by the bull—fertility rituals were celebrated.

As a symbol, the bull, Taurus, corresponds to the yin prin-ciple, the feminine; Aries, the ram, corresponds to the yang prin-ciple, the masculine. Both are horned, male animals. Yet al-though associated with the feminine, the bull, Taurus, is the far larger and more impressive animal. The concepts "masculine" and "feminine" imply no value judgments but rather distinguish fun-damentally different, mutually conditioning and complementary qualities.

Speaking astrologically, the Sun is "exalted" in Aries, i.e., it is especially "strong"; in Taurus, the Moon is "exalted," it has an energy field appropriate to it. In the sign of the bull, Taurus, growth is found in every respect, on the organic and on the psy-chic level. Likewise, growth is related to the moon. In observing the zodiac, we again recognize the general law of energy of which we spoke in connection with the various phases of the Moon and the relationship of the Sun and the Moon: one movement always brings about the countermovement, one impulse the counterim-pulse. We can observe this in the sequence of Aries and Taurus, and the same will be repeated in sequence with the remaining signs of the zodiac. We can look at them all as pairs of counter-vailing tendencies or forces. Through the sequence of tension–re-lease–new tension, we sense the dynamic in which the course of the year comes to pass.

Where Aries is swift, moves by leaps and bounds, and presses forward, Taurus is ponderous, slow of pace, solid and sure-footed on the Earth, but clumsy in high places and on steep hillsides where Aries feels very much at home. Taurus especially enjoys lying on the Earth in the sun. He eats nothing but plants, selectively seeking out the tastiest and enjoying his food by chewing his cud.

Taurus is peaceable and lets others graze next to him as long as there is room and enough to eat. He becomes angry and bellicose only when he is irritated or when he must defend his property. Then, certainly, his attack can be deadly. His great weight (up to 1,700 pounds) lends his attack the necessary impetus.

But in general, his image reflects a nearly passive existence, an image of incorporating and enjoying or of patiently working if a stronger will prompts him. Then he can be tenacious and persevering. For humankind, possession of the bull (Taurus) ·signifies riches, strength, and power (as a draft animal and beast of burden), security, and nourishment. People have found in him everything that gives life a secure foundation.

In his mere appearance, his size, the good proportions of his shape in which everything is sturdy and powerful without seeming heavyset, he is the essence of strength but also of beauty filled with power. Brehm speaks of the "most beautiful proportions of his physical form," of "perfected, integrated beauty."

Consequently, it is not especially astonishing that Venus is the planet that is assigned to the sign Taurus. Beneath her feet, Homer tells us, the Earth starts to sprout and blossom; she spreads pleasure and joi de vivre around her. All the animals follow Venus, who radiates love of life and delight in procreation; the goddesses of growth were most intimately associated with her.

In the image of Taurus, as of Venus, people experienced the delight of enjoyment, peace, harmony, love of the Earth, of nature, and of all natural growth. Thus, the element earth was assigned to this sign of the zodiac. If the natural "gifts" are disturbed, both natures turn into their opposites. If Taurus is provoked, his blind rage knows no limits. Despising death, he attacks even the most powerful predators—and usually comes out victorious. Similar things are said of Venus: if she is offended or slighted, she can avenge herself devastatingly.

Psychically, Taurus qualities are experienced as earthy: proximity to the Earth, to nature, to one's own body; closeness to all processes of growth, which are constant, slow processes. Likewise, the essence of Taurus is cautious and slow. Impatience can seize an attacking Aries when he ought to pay attention to Taurus's tempo. But if one gives Taurus time—psychically and physically—he will reach the goal in his own good time and often with greater intensity and emphasis than many another, for he remains faithful, natural, and genuine and the fruit he harvests is fully ripe.

Naturally here, too, there is a very wide range of levels of actualization. Taurus, like Venus, can lead a fundamentally dull, boring, or apathetic life that exhausts itself in sensual enjoyment and material well-being. Taurus, like Venus, is related to reality and close to the sensual: by feeling, smelling, seeing, tasting, and hearing, they take the world into themselves. And if the obstacles are not too great, they like to deal with it creatively. The "how" depends on the individual endowment.

When Taurus meets with resistances, there are various possibilities of reaction: perhaps he feels spurred on really to prevail, not to relent in his intentions, not to surrender any of his turf, to fulfill his desires. On the other hand, he may avoid reaction as long as he can "for the sake of peace" but actually because it is more comfortable. Then, at most, he shows passive resistance or passive endurance.

Neither Taurus nor Venus knows great ambition (other psychic functions must awaken it). They do not desire to storm any heights, but they can grow toward the heights and then stand there before the world, or before themselves, with inner security, with naturalness, and also with great gravity or significance.

Shadow aspects of Taurus qualities appear if Taurus cannot, will not, or may not affirm his nature; if he cannot give himself time with his inner or outer processes; if his goals cannot grow and mature in him but are forced or suppressed. Then, instead of inner certainty and stability, there is lack of independence, immaturity, and submissiveness to authority. He remains credulous, dependent, in order not to have to be active. He doesn't look obstacles in the eye; that is, he represses what he could feel and see. He can become a Philistine, a hedonist of the moment and of its eternal repetition. Then, collecting and possession of things takes the place of creative, fruitful strength and growth. Possession becomes more important than inner value. Having overpowers being.

The zodiacal sign Taurus is associated with the bodily areas of neck and shoulders. It is sometimes said of someone that he is "bull-headed." Usually, this is not intended as flattery but rather refers to apathy, lack of differentiation, coarseness, and stubbornness. And in fact, the bull's neck and shoulders are particularly impressive. They form the highest point of the bull's body when standing, are especially broad and powerful, and single it out as a draft animal and beast of burden. But what a load a Taurus person can bear!

In body language, a person's ability to bear a burden is often revealed in the way he holds his neck and shoulders. A "genuine" or a healthy bull will only swallow or carry what suits him. He is choosy, sure of instinct, and has good taste. If one swallows everything, it will not agree with him. A strong Taurus likes to take on a lot, but he also notices when it gets to be too much: his neck and shoulder muscles get tense. If he doesn't take this symptom seriously, and if he isn't more careful about his burdens—that is, more conscious—the tension can lead to very painful symptoms. But rightly understood, their intention is only to lead him out of carelessness, insensitivity, or cowardice and coax him toward real battle, to natural joy of life, where Venus is also integrated.

Only where the Venus principle, the psychic relationship to the physical processes, has been neglected, where harmony and good proportion have not been preserved, must body language become so clear that it brings about changes of emotional attitude.

Gemini

Planet Mercury
May 22—June 21

The year is already far advanced when the Sun stands in the sign Gemini. Gemini stands between spring and summer. Soon the longest days will come; vegetation stands in full flower and still it is not yet summer. It is a time between: time of the twins, Gemini, presummer.

The symbol of the twins, Gemini, is the first sign of the zodiac not represented by an animal but by human figures. The symbol is of two persons, two brothers, most intimately bound together, like two sides of a whole.

After the fiery ram, Aries, and the earthy bull, Taurus, the sign of the twins, Gemini, is the first air sign. It is assigned to the mental realm. It is as though now, for the first time, it is important to raise to consciousness what previously had taken place and been experienced physically and psychically. This effort calls for the specifically human function of consciousness, the possibility of reflection, of attitude. Hence, the pair of brothers is especially "fitting" as the sign of the zodiac for the transition from spring to the summer solstice.

From the earliest times, twins have moved humankind as "something special." Early on they acquired symbolic significance, and in many religions they play a role, be it in human or animal form. Since the two prominent, very brightly shining, fixed stars of this constellation acquired the names Castor and Pollux, I shall follow the myth told about them. But I will also draw on the older Greek tale that arose when the constellation was called only "the Twins." In both versions are features that illuminate the essence of the sign and also offer a good foundation for later reflections.

The constellation of the twins was an image of unique fraternal love and depicted the value of an intimate blood relationship (Schadewaldt 1956, p. 46). Castor and Pollux were twins, sons of Leda, but not sired by the same father. Only Pollux was a true son of Zeus and immortal. Castor was sired the same night by King Tyndareos and was mortal. The love of the two brothers was so great that Pollux asked his father, Zeus, to let him die as Castor would so that they would remain united even in death. Zeus allowed them to remain together and stay alternately on Olympus or in Hades. Thus, they came into the domains of various gods of light, they alternated from light to dark and were the only beings who participated in both worlds. For humankind, they were heroes and rescuers in times of need, and they are supposed to have possessed this gift as celestial gods who again and again survived the descent into the dark, the journey into night and death.

It is not astonishing that Mercury is assigned to Gemini, the twins, when we recall that he alone among the planetary gods could be the messenger between Olympus and Hades, he alone had access to the realm of the dead and guided the deceased thither.

The older myth of Gemini, pertaining to the constellation, tells of a Theban pair of twins (Schadewaldt 1956, p. 47n.).[22] Zeus had made love with the beautiful Antiope. When she discovered that she was pregnant, she became frightened of her stern father and had to flee. Everybody made an attempt on her life, but she succeeded in secretly giving birth to her two sons and entrusting them to a cowherd who reared them. After many years of captivity Antiope was able to free herself, and she sought her sons in the area where she had left them. Mercury helped her, leading her to the right trail, and he commanded her pursuer to relinquish his regency over the city of Thebes to the two twins. Mercury then ordered the twins to surround the undefended city with a strong wall. Both went to work, but in very different ways, for as much as they loved each other, they were also very different. The one was strongly built, a skilled laborer, and exerted his full strength procuring the boulders for building the wall. He invented techniques for lifting and piling them. The other brother, slight of build and contemplative, had learned no craft from Mercury, but he had received a lyre and had learned to play divinely. When he played and sang, praising the gods, trunks of trees and great cliffs moved of themselves and harmoniously arranged themselves in layers. What gives a crude wall its solid construction is the structure, a spiritual principle that, in Greek, was called *harmonia*.

The myth itself positions Mercury in relationship to the twins. He saves them and instructs them in how they must delimit and secure their future realm. Each of them, according to his inner nature, finds his path to self-realization: the one through manual skill, clever reflection, and employment of his best resources; the other in a mental and spiritual way, through intuitive insight into the relationships of sounds and numbers and in the laws of harmony, and perhaps also thanks to a little diplomacy, such as Mercury himself utilized when he played and sang so magnificently for Apollo. All these are Mercury's gifts, which determine the nature of the twins, Gemini.

As an image of psychic possibilities, the two legends of the Gemini show that persons can experience themselves from such different sides, gifted with such different possibilities, that it seems they must be the offspring of two sets of parents. The interests, inclinations, and abilities of the Gemini person are manifold and divergent. Even with the most earnest efforts directed toward uniting the various potentials, the Gemini person will not easily find peace: the path leads from Olympus to Hades and back again, alternating heights and depths, light and dark. All of Mercury's means and ways are available to the Gemini; but, like Mercury, they are also always on the go, never completely at home anywhere. They can be seized by restlessness but also be intellectually moved, physically agile; they can be "on the go" in the most diverse ways. It is as though the Gemini always have four eyes, four arms and legs at their disposal, as though they saw more than others or saw hidden things at the same time, as though everywhere they had to undertake something. There is always something new to learn or to teach; the Gemini are like Mercury on the first day of his conquest of the world. Enterprising spirit; mobility; love of contact with siblings, acquaintances, relatives; intellectual and practical interests are his gifts. The Gemini person is not confronted with the question: Should I do this *or* that? but with the problem: How can I do this *and* that, too? It is the task of Gemini to discover one's own essence and then remain true to it, just as each of the very different twin brothers

pursued his activities wholeheartedly. Or the Gemini will have to find a rhythm in which various interests receive their due: the depths and the heights at their times, or practical activity and intellectual pursuits in the appropriate rhythm. The Gemini's path must follow Heraclitus's motto: following two paths, the path downward and the path upward, that together are one path. An image for this is Hermes's staff with the two snakes, one descending, the other ascending.

Shadow aspects of Gemini have already made their appearance: inner unrest, inconstancy, the temptation to begin much and finish little, wanting to learn a lot but not really immersing oneself deeply in anything; hurrying from one thing to another without considering either the ascent to the heights or the necessity of descent. Here, the original experience of "twin possibilities" that live in the image of both myths as well as in the figure of Mercury—coming to terms with matter and spirit, life and death, heights and depths—are neglected. Especially today, the shadow aspects of the Gemini nature stand out: unrest, fragmentation, superficiality, perpetual mobility that tarries nowhere and that has no care for fundamental meaning.

In the body, the zodiacal sign Gemini is associated with the lungs and respiration. In the breath are "two sorts of gifts": in inhalation and exhalation an exchange between inside and outside takes place. It is a giving and taking and giving again. Among other gases, we inhale oxygen that plants exhale, take it into our blood and, among other gases, exhale carbon dioxide that plants need. The process of respiration signifies exchange but also our dependence on others, the complementary side of nature (corresponding to the image of the twins, Gemini).

We are familiar with superficial breathing and with deep breathing. The one reveals nervousness, excitement, or weakness. The other leads to rest, concentration, to deepening and strengthening. The latter is something the "Gemini soul" often very much needs.

Cancer

Planet Moon
June 22—July 22

Following the various facets of the Sun in Aries and Taurus, new ones appear in the zodiacal sign of the twins, Gemini, whose nature it is to be on the go, in motion, to conquer the world, to strive for contradictory things and, if possible, to unite them. On June 22, the Sun attains its zenith and enters the sign Cancer.[23] This is again a cardinal sign and a special moment in the Sun's movement. The solstice takes place in this segment of the ecliptic. Here, between the ascending and descending movements, lies a moment of hesitation, a pause; from our perspective, a gradual reverse movement occurs before the Sun continues on its course, now toward the lower half of the sphere of Earth.

The countermovement to the upward-striving sign Gemini comes not only from the course of the Sun but equally in the symbolic animal of the zodiacal sign Cancer, the crab. While Gemini moves with four legs at once in different directions, Cancer the crab usually has more than four *pairs* of legs available, but it moves slowly nevertheless. Cancer lives in the depths, in the water, almost immobile. It approaches everything cautiously and draws back if it meets obstacles or dangers. In its camouflaged color, it is adapted to its surroundings and behaves very inconspicuously or withdraws to hidden places.

Concretely, the crab, Cancer, belongs to the element water. It lives in rivers or in the sea. In the "inner" quality, it also represents the realm of the waters, of the depths, the soul dimension, the realm of emotion, and ultimately the unconscious, corresponding to the "essence" of the planet that is assigned to it, the Moon.

It may seem odd that the Sun's highest point of ascent is associated not with the Sun but with the Moon. But the cardinal point of the solstice is not only a zenith; it is at the same time the beginning of a descent into the depths, the beginning of "death." Here we are concerned with change, with increase and decrease, with reversal. We experience this change in exemplary manner in the Moon.

The intellectual connections with the animal that became the symbol extend yet further. We are all familiar with the crab's claws, with which it seizes and holds fast, with which it can crush its food and even defend itself. We are also reminded of its compound eyes and the two feelers, its antennae, and that it wears an armor of chitin joining head and thorax. It is perhaps less well known that the crab must slough its shell repeatedly in order to grow, and thus its development is a transformation. The crab larva already has many limbs on its head and thorax, but no shell and no claws. Growth is always linked with threat and the proximity of death, for while it is shedding its shell, the animal is without armor and hence without any sort of protection. The compound eyes and the antennae enable the crab to react rapidly to anything in its environment. But without its armor, it is mortally vulnerable.

The psychic significance of the various phases of the Moon may be an obvious analogy to the crab's transformations: the open crescent which corresponds to the child's dependence on the mother can be seen in the relationship to the unprotected, shell-less life phase of the crab, while the full moon refers to the psychically matured, "complete" person and corresponds to the well-protected crab in its armor.

According to Greek legend, at the time of the full moon, the crab, Cancer, responding to Hera's call, climbed up out of the waters of the Lernaian swamp and bit Hercules in the heel because Hera had a grudge against him.[24] Thereupon Hercules crushed the unpleasant creature underfoot and the multitude of insignificant stars was created. The full moon phase of the crab was past; a new crab with a new shell had to be formed. Again and again, it must surrender its armor, must accept suffering; otherwise growth, maturation, and transformation are not possible.

We experience this form of transformation also on the psychic plane in Cancer as an "inner" sign of the zodiac. The starting point is lack of protection, vulnerability: emotional suppleness and impressionability, a condition of being exposed to the world unprotected. There exists in the beginning, and again and again, an emotional nakedness. It begets fear and the need for protection.

But the absence of the armor can also be felt as openness to emotional experience, extending to the point of feeling completely delivered over to it. Every event, every movement, continues to work aftereffects in Cancer. The realm in which Cancer is at home is the domain of the emotions. Cancer's openness is an openness inward, to the inner world (whereas Gemini was open toward the outer world, extraverted). Cancer has "antennae" for psychic movements and a lively relationship to fantasies and dreams. But Cancer also needs armor when he approaches reality and the demands of the outer world.

The best protective covering at the beginning of life, and again in times of developmental steps and inner transformations, is the attention and warmth of other people. The image of the mother, the friend, the lover appears. But ultimately Cancer must have his own armor. He develops this through an increasing capacity to adapt, even in a sort of emotional diplomacy that consists of surrounding himself with people who are well disposed to him, who perhaps even need him. If he places his sensitivity and knowledge of how easily we can be wounded in the service of others (as therapist, minister, or in social service), he can serve and feel strong at the same time.

Family offers Cancer a great refuge and support. But here the danger is that he will cling to it so much that he will not release what his pincers hold; for example, he will not be able to separate from the parental home. Or he binds others to himself: the partner, the children. People who were not "released" by their parents often complain of this.

In other ways, too, the longing for conservation and preservation underlies Cancer's emotional attitude: he loves tradition, early memories, the family relationships, and holds fast to many things in pictures and notes.

What Cancer fears is criticism and attack. He is ill suited for battle in public life. He much prefers to back off. He avoids confrontations even among friends and prefers to flee hard realities. He avoids conflict or contact for as long as possible. His first escape is into fantasies, daydreams, beloved activities in familiar areas where he feels protected and at home. Like the armor, softness is also part of Cancer's nature; feeling his way forward and drawing back; the wish to hold onto and to preserve as well as the clearly sensed demand to give up everything—the entire old protective husk—again and again.

Shadow aspects emerge when Cancer is not aware of his own nature, when he wants to conceal his anxiousness and timidity from himself and from the world about him. Then he can confuse fear of humiliation with modesty, disguise his own anxiousness with solicitude for others, mistake flight from reality for introversion, idle play for the muse's gift. He will be offended and feel neglected but will never have let his needs or expectations be known. He will haggle with the harsh world around him, which he does not correctly recognize because he always avoids it. When he helps others in order to help himself, he can mistake self-satisfaction for devotion or self-sacrifice.

If, on the other hand, Cancer is conscious of his basic structure, he will approach the demands of the outer world again and again, "sense" with the help of his antennae what he can take on, and seize and work over with his powerful pincers what he can cope with and make his own. He will have to be prepared for the anxieties of liminality and learn to overcome them, will have to practice letting go but at other times also firmly seize what is essential to him and gives him meaning, and he will have to be faithful to this decision.

In the bodily realm, Cancer is assigned to the stomach. As image, it corresponds to the open crescent of the Moon into which everything falls, whether digestible or not. Foods are held in the stomach until they have been processed with digestive juices so that they can be moved on for further digestion. Many of the expectations, disappointments, unbearable and burdensome things that Cancer must swallow remain long undigested, oppressive, and painful. If transformation succeeds, growth and maturation is possible. If it does not succeed, there are difficulties, for example, ulcers.

Leo

Planet Sun
July 22—August 22

With the zodiacal sign Cancer, the Sun reached its zenith. Yet, it is as though the soul—and nature—needs a while longer to savor the full abundance, to plunge into it, in order to absorb and to radiate what the Sun's full strength has brought about. Now the strong, masculine lion, the solar animal and representative of the yang principle, confronts the intensely impressionable and subtly reacting crab, the new moon crescent or the yin principle.

The lion used to be at home in the entire Mediterranean region and was revered everywhere as the royal, indeed the divine, animal. In Egypt, it was considered the manifest form of the sun god. As the god of the morning Sun, Horus could assume a lion's head. The lion symbolized the all-seeing eye of the Sun because, even in sleep, it supposedly never closed its eyes. In the cult of Mithras, too, the Sun was symbolized by the lion. According to legend, only he who himself is leonine and solar can vanquish a lion, as Hercules vanquished the Nemean lion. In the lion's den, the lion spared Daniel of the Old Testament because "another Sun" ruled in his heart. Whoever does not carry a countervailing Sun within is handed over to death in the sign of the Lion, Leo, since the Sun as a star cannot only enliven but, if the intensity is too great, also scorch, indeed, kill.

Thanks to its impressive figure, the powerful mane, the loud roar, and its strength, the lion is especially respected and feared by man and beast. The lion belongs to the wild cats and, aside from its strength, is also distinguished by its vigilance. The lion became the symbolic guardian of temples and palaces and the quintessence of rulership in general. Regulus, the largest fixed star in Leo, the constellation of the lion, is called "regal."

Aside from mating season, the lion lives solitarily and claims a certain territory as its own. It is not possible for many lions to live together because they need too much food. At night, the lion goes hunting and takes whatever lures it to the chase, even other large predators. During the day, it lies peaceably in the sun. If other animals approach, it drives them away with a commanding roar.

Following the preceding cardinal sign, the new beginning, change of direction, and beginning of a new quadrant, the lion, Leo, represents a fixed sign: security, satisfaction with the condition now attained (as did Taurus, the bull, in the preceding quadrant).

The zodiacal sign Leo is a fire sign. Where the fiery element in Aries found expression as impulsiveness, readiness to jump, and as a dynamic enterprising spirit, the fiery element in Leo is the solar energy we have described: strength, dynamism in movement, and in potential energy; here the fire is warmth and radiance.

In the psychic realm, this force finds expression as vital energy, as active mastery of the world in optimism and confidence. Here, the expression of a strong will and a self-assurance taken completely for granted belong to the fiery impulse. But this self-assurance presupposes the ego's consciousness of its own identity: "I am I," as we described in regard to the Sun symbol. Persons who feel themselves determined by "Leo qualities" are strong, sure, watchful, and possesses formative powers. They experience themselves as a totality, with their own intentions, their own will, and with the consciousness of disposable physical and psychic energy.

Leo stakes out his territory very precisely and is alert so that no foreign influences creep in. Inner, psychic independence and independence in external affairs are close to Leo's heart and increase his feeling of freedom and self-worth. He approaches his environment and his fellow man openly, loves confrontation, and especially loves to make appearances. He is not much concerned with experiencing how others feel or whether perhaps they are suffering, let alone empathizing or helping by feeling himself into their situation, as does Cancer. He prefers to hear that others are doing well and radiates his optimism, his cordiality and confidence upon them. Above all, he feels best this way.

In the astrological sign Leo—as in all the other signs— there exists not only a strong relation between the sign and the associated planet (the psychic quality of expression), but almost an identity. At times Leo and Sun can be used as synonyms, yet there is a decisive difference: Leo hunts at night and sleeps during the day. In the myth of Helios, on the other hand, the Sun sleeps when it travels back toward the east at night with the four-horse hitch in the boat through the depths of Oceanus. The Sun and Leo complement each other, forming a totality into a never completely extinguished consciousness, never-ending energy, presence, dynamism. But this also means that the dark side cannot be seen, not even by Leo himself. He avoids emotional problems, he doesn't like the night side of the soul. He is devoted only to the Sun side, to the rational perception of problems and to active intervention. Hence, he does not always turn out to be a good judge of his fellow man. He treats the emotional conflicts of others with good-natured humor or with a certain indifference; but at the same time he can be cordial, actively "give the other a boost," and show himself to be magnanimous. But afterward he again turns away to other interests.

For strong partners, a Leo is one of the most pleasant and encouraging companions, for he is self-assured and self-satisfied. Weaker natures experience him as "tyrant," as an "authority," as the "patriarch" who is unwilling to share the domain of his power, and Leo then feels bored. It is his nature to take possession of his domain, be it his family or in private or professional life, and as long as he is not disturbed, he is peaceable.

Depending on circumstances, he will openly listen to criticism or magnanimously pass over it. Only with difficulty can he admit weaknesses or shadow aspects because he "doesn't have any." Whatever he is unwilling to see, he does not see. If he does something disgraceful, he can laugh at himself or just brush it aside and repress it. Thus, he makes banal vital topics not infrequently. He cannot get into feelings (that *also* would be necessary when dealing with the topic), for he does not want to lose any of his self-assurance. As a lover, Leo is hearty, fiery, dynamic, but

Leo

finds closeness burdensome and constricting. Thus, the way he treats or leaves or distances himself from a beloved person or object can have a brutal effect. As a partner, he likes to be virile, but he is not empathetic, and not infrequently he despises anyone who engages completely. This holds true for both men and women.

Leo can have a boundless sense of entitlement but also give magnanimously and "thank cordially." Or he will give like a benefactor—and forget to thank for gifts received. Our shadow sides are just those characteristics that lie in the shade, that is, that are unknown to us, of which we are unconscious. In the case of Leo, they result from his proud sense of himself and from what he wills himself not to see and therefore "overlooks." Natural pride can turn into vanity. Hedonism replaces the joy or meaning of life that Leo has let slip through his fingers. Hardheartedness arises where he does not admit his own feelings or the closeness of another, patronizing where empathy is not possible. Hedonism also conceals the fear of death. Boundless demands on life arise when he is unwilling to see the meaning of life or when he cannot admit it because it is "loaded with feelings."

How vehemently the response of this sign is to the themes announced by the earlier signs! How vehemently one energetic impulse reacts to another. Here again we see with especial clarity that only movement and countermovement yield a totality, only Cancer and Leo, Moon and Sun, create a basis upon which further development is possible, be it in life or in relation to the zodiac.

In the body, Leo, like the Sun—and it cannot be otherwise—is assigned to the heart, the central organ upon whose functioning our entire physical life depends.

Since ancient times, people have "known" that the heart is the real seat of the will to live and of vital energy. Whoever dies of a "broken heart" really doesn't want to live any longer. Whoever experiences "heartache" must become alert to his "heart's desires," which are not receiving their due, which are getting too little attention.

It is part of the Leo nature that one is too proud to spare oneself, that one overestimates one's strength, that one boundlessly makes plans, strives, gives of oneself—to the point of heart failure.

Virgo

Planet Mercury
August 23—September 22

Following impulse and counter-impulse, we again encounter a period of working through, reflection and anticipation, of equilibration. The Sun's course leads through the sign of the virgin, Virgo, whose planet is again Mercury. The period of the highest abundance has passed. The harvest has begun and is still being gathered in. The Sun no longer has the strength that it radiated only a month earlier, and in Virgo itself self-assurance and confidence are no longer as strong as they were in Leo.

What was first heard in Cancer only now becomes clear: death belongs to life, depth to height, decrease follows abundance. But it is also a time of "not yet," of "not yet completely." We can still rejoice in the fruits, the grape is just now being harvested. Now it is especially delectable and good to make the most

119

of time. The fruits of previous experiences must be sorted and ordered. Mercury is now the function that is used most urgently: for the purpose of efficacious action as well as for careful and thorough pondering and securing.

The symbolic image of this sign of the zodiac is the virgin, Virgo; the primary star of this sign is Spica, the ear of corn. The sign ♍ is an abbreviation of the Greek word for virgin, *parthenos*: παρθενοσ, πρ. In Hellenistic times, people believed Athena was this virgin because she had the epithet *parthenos* (her temple is the Parthenon on the Acropolis). But Athena, with the olive branch, less befits this goddess than Demeter and Kore, whose symbol was the ear of corn or head of grain. At the climax of the celebration of the Eleusinian mysteries, a head of grain was held aloft: this *is* Demeter, this *is* Persephone, the one is the other. This is also Kore, the grain maiden who is still a virgin. And the good tidings hidden within this was: this is you, this is me.

The head of grain or ear of corn simultaneously contains both the fruit and the seed: harvest of what has been, seed for future life. But, as we saw when discussing Kore/Persephone, part of this has to do with the descent into the depths, sacrifice to the underworld, entering into the dark in order to be able again to ascend to the light and bring new fertility.

There is something compelling, dignified, or moving about the figure of the virgin, Virgo, depending on how one views her. She is fully developed but untouched, unviolated. She is not womanly like Venus, not yielding, sensuous. Hence, Venus is not her planet either. Virgo is still chaste because she herself has not yet awakened to her womanly and maternal potential. Or she is virgin by cult and religious vocation. Abstinence can be seen as a prerequisite for the accumulation of energy that is necessary for an enthusiastic encounter with the deity or for prophetic talents (as in the instance of the sibyls and vestals). Virginity can also be a voluntary sacrifice in order to be better able to bring her own possibilities into play or into battle (as did Joan of Arc).

Virginity in this sense is not restricted only to women. Each person participates in that aspect of the Sun symbolized in this zodiacal sign. There is chastity, abstinence, or self-denial in men as well as women, along with the other tendencies and characteristics that belong to the symbol of the zodiacal sign. It is in the nature of the virgin to limit herself, not to pour herself out, not to give. Virgo must employ her possibilities and powers consciously. She places herself in the service of a task or an idea, she would like or must encounter very concrete tasks.

Virgo is an earth sign. But in this sign, one can no longer, as in Taurus, naively encounter matter or reality, let it come one's way, and live and be absorbed in the moment. Here, the harvest must be carefully administered and utilized. It is a question of looking ahead, foresight, of anticipatory cleverness, as in the case of the seven clever virgins who took care of their lamps and kept them burning until the bridegroom came.

What Virgo must accomplish would not be possible without the influence of Mercury. Here the task is to separate the useful from the useless, sift chaff from wheat. It is a question of rationalizing the work in the physical, psychic, and intellectual realms, for the powers that are still at one's disposal must be used economically. Virgo needs a plan before she begins the work. She needs methods, foundations, a precise organization so that all that is superfluous or disadvantageous is avoided. That is Mercury's function: working out systems, classifications, statistics, exercises, preparations, and test runs.

In the psychic realm, from the point of view of the "inner zodiac," Virgo is sensitive or touchy, can be disturbed by trivialities, even thrown into confusion by the disruption of cherished habits. Virgo is hesitant and familiar with a degree of caution bordering on suspiciousness when investigating whether something can or cannot be assimilated. Virgo behaves as if reticent. For the sake of self-protection, she preserves a distance whenever strangers get too close. She has a strong sense for sympathy and antipathy but prefers to hold back in critical emotional areas. This is often ascribed to "emotional modesty" but is really nothing more than "emotional economy."

To Virgo's practical and intellectual precision belongs the maxim: one may do and think only what fully corresponds to one's personal uniqueness. This leads to an almost compulsive precision, to an overly sensitive morality, to pedantry (in the physical as in the psychic realm). Virgo has an antipathy to all that is superfluous, unkempt, and unclear. Things are most uncomplicated for Virgo when they involve executing concrete tasks properly and efficiently. Then Virgo plunges in with joy. Mercury carries out the task to the point of mastery, of copious knowledge and broad, professional ability. This can manifest as easily in perfectly maintained accounts as in magnificent scholarly research work.

Shadow aspects creep in when, for example, Virgo is too fearful of overextension. Overextension can be experienced as the demands of another, although sometimes the feeling arises from insufficient consciousness of Virgo's compulsive drive for perfection. Virgo feels so easily disturbed and thrown off balance because she would like never to disturb anybody. Virgo likes to make out that the poor behavior of others is responsible for her own ill humors and dissatisfaction. Thus, she can be very intolerant toward others but, on the other hand, self-righteous because she considers herself always to be reticent and modest.

Feeling sorry for herself or nagging dissatisfaction have their supposed source in lack of physical well-being or being overworked, but this often conceals a suppressed wish for human closeness, for surrender to another, the wish and the longing not only to become absorbed in a thing but to be seized by deep experience. Such is the way traversed by Kore/Persephone and which faces Virgo as a possibility, with the head of grain, the *spica*, that she holds in her hand.

Since Persephone's path led into the depths, Virgo's hesitation is understandable, likewise, the anxious holding back, indeed refusal, or the drive to keep her distance from everything, not to be robbed, meaning not to be robbed of her self-possession, uniqueness, or her factual spirit.

The bodily area assigned to Virgo are the intestines. In the metaphorical sense, this will be obvious to everybody: here food is digested and assimilated so that it can serve the entire organism as sustenance. This is Virgo's activity, translated into another image. Here it can be a question of processing what has been harvested, of food. But we also think of processing in the intellectual sense, in the sense of Mercury; of a transformation of perceived facts into cumulative knowledge and systematic thought structures or of perceiving or intuiting that, in the further course of life, it is a question of the soul's transformation, of the readiness to turn toward higher goals or greater depths.

Likewise, in a concrete sense, we can often establish a relationship between the capacity to digest physical as well as psychic burdens and bodily health, or, on the other hand, we note digestive disorders of the most varied sort.

Libra

Planet Venus
September 23—October 22

With the Sun's entrance into the sign of Libra, we reach the autumnal equinox. Now the same light relationships exist as did on March 21, but how different is the mood at the beginning of autumn!

Again and again, people have assumed that the sign of Libra arose purely from the calendar and was to be understood as the sign of balance between light and dark, as the sign of cosmic equilibrium between the two halves of the year.

As a constellation, Libra, the scales, was known already in early times in ancient Mesopotamia and Babylon. Sometimes the Greeks and the Egyptians also depicted the constellation being held, sometimes by a male and sometimes by a female figure. This alone shows that the psyche was not satisfied with the superficial parallel to the calendar. Likewise, appointing Venus to this sign indicates other intuitions or experiences that may have led to the image of the scales, Libra, as a facet of the Sun symbol.

The sign of Libra forms the counterpart to the sign of Aries. Libra is also a cardinal sign: a new quadrant begins. But where Aries, the ram, represented the fiery element, Libra, the scales, belongs to the element air. Aries, the ram, leaps toward the light, into life. With Libra, the air sign, the soul responds in a mental, spiritual manner: by pondering, weighing. If there is to be a balance to urgent Mars, Venus must answer in Libra. This transpires in the sense of a considered, cautious opening toward another; or it appears as a backward glance at things past and a pondering of the future.

If something is placed on one pan of the scales, a counterweight is needed on the other pan so that there will be equilibrium again. As a psychic function, Venus is concerned with reconciliation, harmony, exchange, and communication. Or, seen in a different way, in the sign of Libra the psyche responds to the demands of the outer world in part by weighing them and, if possible, agreeing to them; but, on the other hand, it is concerned with the balance between the demands of the outer world and inner demands and needs.

In Libra, Venus is more prudent, cautious, ponders things more, and perhaps is more calculating, more conscious than in the sensuous Taurus existence. Here, it is no longer a question of bodily well-being, material possession, of warmth and natural bonds with everything that pleases Venus. Here, it is above all a question of the right proportions in communication, of articulated, harmonious relationships, of equanimity. These are gifts of Venus and conditions such as Libra desires. But since these are not guaranteed and cannot be secured possessions but must be attained ever and again, Libra's equanimity is quite labile.

The image of the scales holds still more motifs. Since time immemorial, this sign of the zodiac at the point of transition from the light to the dark phase has contained references to the scales of fate: things are weighed to see what will endure, what will be of permanent value.

Zeus, we are told in the *Iliad* (Homer 22.208–213), weighed the lot of death. Even Hermes weighed the souls (e.g., of Achilles and Patroclus). The scales of fate are also known from

the Egyptian judgment of the dead; we encounter it in Tibet and among other peoples of the ancient world. Already around 3000 B.C.E., an image of Osiris with a balance scale in his hand had been sculpted. Later, the Egyptian god Anubis weighed, in one pan of a balance scale, the heart of the deceased (which was seen as the seat of the soul and of reason) and, on the other, the feather of truth. The heart had to be found neither too light nor too heavy. The soul must be in balance with its inner truth. It befits the element air in the sign of Libra that the heart is weighed against a feather, against the spirit of truth. The Old Testament also reports the weighing of the soul. There, the "mene tekel u-pharsim" means that the heart of the king is counted, weighed, and found too light (Daniel 5:25–28).

In Libra, the Sun begins its descent toward the southern hemisphere. It is the turning point toward the gradual predominance of the dark. This moment also demands a gradual turn toward the dark or shadow side of life; it demands a new emotional attitude, a weighing of what is now important and unimportant, a conscious attitude toward the values of life, a conscious answer to the demands of the outer world but also to the dark or burdensome demands.

Here Venus's psychic qualities are needed. Venus was a match for stormy Mars and lovingly received him. Again and again, a strong Venus will be a match for powerful demands. Then harmony between demand and fulfillment, giving and taking, can come about. Here it is a question of meeting one great weight with a correspondingly great counterweight. Then even burdensome darkness can finally be accepted. But when one does this, one must also examine and weigh what demands are justified and what the values are that the heart is allowing to live on.

Libra in us (corresponding to the inner zodiac) demands harmony, structured balance between inner and outer worlds as well as in interpersonal relationships. Here, the need for unanimity can be so great that one prefers to renounce deep feelings rather than run into disharmony or conflict. One would prefer to remain polite, and that means noncommittal, rather than surrender oneself to the onerous process of coming to terms with the situation. Most of all, Libra loves to say "yes"; whenever a refusal, a rejection, is necessary, Libra does it with difficulty and often only later, if possible perhaps by phone, and always in friendly terms.

Libra suffers if he sees himself compelled to make decisions and experiences this everywhere, in great as in small things. This suffering is of such a sort that other people find it difficult to feel their way into it: it seem like an inner compulsion, a decision well-considered and yet seemingly made too soon that has to be taken back later. External pressures, the urgings of others, hinder Libra in easily making a decision that is genuinely his. The outer world seduces Libra to deeds that run counter to all better judgment. Or it seduces Libra to delegate his own responsibility to others.

If they have not already appeared, shadow aspects now come into view. Where Libra ponders but does not dare, the consequences are avoidance, weakness in conflicts, ambivalence, overadaptation. Many view this side of Libra as "peaceableness," indeed as "love of peace." But the obliging "protectiveness" of one's fellows conceals a protectiveness of oneself. And with all his surface friendliness, behind his elegant detachment, Libra often hides a fear of letting feelings move him because they might overwhelm him and disturb his equilibrium. Even a small weight on one side of the scales can evoke an intense swing on the other. Therefore, Libra unconsciously withdraws from emotional stress situations by withdrawing from feelings.

This is how, with great composure and lack of involvement, Libra protects himself or herself against too great closeness and the emotional demands of others.

These shadow aspects appear especially when the ego is not conscious. Libra mistakenly believes he or she is able to do justice to and hence resolve the demands of life and of the surrounding world by pondering and planning in a diplomatic and courteous way, but ultimately this means without engagement.

This way Libra remains only superficial. No exchange between the heights and the depths takes place; everything dark is excluded.

In the body, Libra is assigned to the kidneys, which free the body from metabolic byproducts. In the kidneys, whatever is harmful to the body is separated out and these substances are eliminated in the urine. If this does not succeed, if there is no "solution," inflammation of the kidneys and kidney stones can develop and lead to unbearable stresses and suffering.

In the sign of Libra, the timely decision must be made as to what is harmful or good for body and soul, and whatever is harmful must be eliminated at the right time so that the correct balance will be maintained. When something affects the kidneys, i.e., a problem cannot be solved, this is a signal to turn intensively to the dark side or still unconscious side of a difficulty that, up until now, was perceived only physically, in order to find a new equilibrium.

Scorpio

Planets Mars and Pluto
October 23—November 21

On October 23, the Sun begins its transit through the sign of Scorpio to which the planet Mars is assigned and, since its discovery in 1930, also the planet Pluto.

Scorpio is the counterpart to the sign of Taurus. While in that fixed sign, certainty was attained for life and the Earth would fulfill all the senses in increasing measure; here in the fixed sign of Scorpio, it becomes a certainty that all living nature will perish. Leaves fall, the sap ebbs. Whatever has not been harvested perishes. On the other hand, winter seeds are sown: while the old dies, new germinations are being prepared.

Concurrent with the external process of "dying," the energies withdraw within or into the depths in physical as in psychic life. The extreme up and down between hope and despair, between affirmation and negation, inspired assent and depressive dejection, fear of dying and the trust in becoming, can be the cause of an extreme inner strife. A corresponding split results from the succession of opposed planets in the zodiac: Mars in Scorpio follows Venus in Libra as though he were lured by her amiability or challenged by her need for balance to disturb it, to break into her peaceful world and fulfill his desire.

The image that gave this sign of the zodiac its name is the scorpion. As a constellation, it is one of the largest and most impressive (although not always visible in the northern hemisphere). The radiant center between head and body—which the Arabs call "the heart"—is the fixed star Antares (80,000 times brighter than the Sun, but 500 light-years distant).

The scorpion belongs to the arachnids (the same group as spiders), measures up to six inches in length, has an unarticulated head and thorax, four pairs of legs for locomotion, one pair of short, small mandibular feelers with jaws, and a pair of long, horizontal prehensile arms. The rear part of the body consists of thirteen segments, decreasing in width, which looks like a tail, and is very mobile. The last segment contains the feared stinger and poison gland. Scorpions are nocturnal animals and live concealed under rocks, the bark of trees, and in caves. They are found in dry regions, in deserts and in the steppe. In Europe, too, there are smaller varieties of scorpions (in Italy, for example). Scorpions eat insects and other arthropods. They catch and crush their prey with their claws. If the animal a scorpion has caught can defend itself, the scorpion uses its stinger and its poison paralyzes or kills the prey. For humans, the sting only of the tropical varieties is deadly, but the sting of any scorpion is very painful.

Scorpio

This image of the scorpion, which can shoot unexpectedly out of a dark hiding place, has always been a symbol for the dangerous, death-dealing powers of darkness. In the Gilgamesh epic, two scorpion men guard the entrance to the underworld. Snake and scorpion are the adversaries of the light god, Mithras: when the primordial steer is sacrificed (a vegetation sacrifice), they attempt albeit in vain to withhold the semen and the blood of the sacrificial animal when the world is formed. The Egyptian goddess Selkis, worshiped in the form of a scorpion, was regarded as the protectress of the living and of the dead.

In the sign of Scorpio, it is a question of a battle between life and death, a battle to reclaim life from death.

The planet traditionally appointed to this sign has always been Mars, and since its discovery, Pluto has also been assigned to Scorpio. At first, this might appear only to be a visualization of the scorpion aspect, but the interconnections run deeper. Fighting and killing is one side of Mars, the one most often mentioned. As the god of war and siege, he was always beloved of Pluto (Hades), for Mars brought him many victims of war and death.

In Aries, Mars brought the impulse for life; in Scorpio, he fights with life, often against life, or for life. Venus in Libra, the opposed sign, responds to Mars's demand in Aries. Here, it is as though Mars in Scorpio braces against the certainty of Venus in Taurus, as if he combated a stubborn satisfaction and the security of an all too comfortable and self-satisfied foundation.

To a special degree, dynamism belongs to Mars. As we have previously recognized, a counterimpulse against the preceding impulse is revealed in each sign of the zodiac; here, too, the powerful dynamism has erupted that was expressly avoided in the sign Libra. With Mars in Scorpio, we enter the depths that have been postulated several times, but more often glimpsed, worked over, and pondered than dared.

Corresponding to the inner zodiac, Scorpio's element is water. That this association is to be understood exclusively in a psychic sense is especially clear here, since the symbolic animal itself lives in arid and hot places. But in the realm of the soul, it is handed over to the surges of all the emotions, follows the waves into the heights as into the depths. "Exulting to heaven, depressed to death," as Goethe, at whose birth the sign Scorpio was rising in the East, aptly expressed it. It is the image of the soul's night sea journey, corresponding to the whale swallowing Jonah, being swept away into the heights and into the depths, but also in ecstasy and intoxication—with the hope, but definitely not with the guarantee, of finding land again at the end.

Fear and terror were the fruit of Mars's and Venus's union: here this is repeated, so to speak, annually, again and again as a lifelong possibility. Venus in Taurus and Mars in Scorpio are, as polar opposites, always related to one another. To them Eros was also born and finally Anteros: love given and love requited, who could develop further only together. Here, in the image of the scorpion, the predominant star is called Antares: contra Mars. The tumultuous, lethally dangerous side of Mars is necessary so that contra Mars, the countervailing force of new life, is also possible. No longer captive to the Earth and to pleasure but departure to perhaps higher goals—this is what Mars in Scorpio can announce.

It is obvious that here there are particularly great differences in the spectrum of what can be experienced. Because darkness ascends in the outer world, the powers of the inner world are increased to the greatest degree of tension. They can be experienced and utilized destructively. They can lead into Pluto's depths, into death, or they can lead to a creative process of change. They demand surrender of old certainties, devotion, and sacrifice. We always experience this as a test that tears us to pieces and awakens the longing to find rest and redemption at last.

In this, great difficulties in the sign of Scorpio are due precisely to the deficient relationship to the outer world. When all energies are concentrated in the psychic realm, they are withdrawn from the outer world. Reality is either not perceived or is misinterpreted on the basis of the subjective experience. This leads to collisions with the *Umwelt,* the environment, above all to difficulties in contact with one's fellows.

Scorpio can scream for help and completion with great persuasiveness. Then he attracts all those like him or those fascinated by his concentrated emotional energy who become, for the time being, his slavish supporters. When he does actually receive help, he often does not even notice it because his emotional hunger is insatiable.

That he can attract, absorb, and exploit the energy of others lies, for Scorpio, in the shadow. He will not express thanks for this because he does not realize it. Thus, he usually overtaxes the patience and devotion of his friends. He may not always have to sting the other mortally in battle. Without noticing it, he perpetually stings others and thus himself, too, for this is how he spoils the best of human contacts for himself.

One form of stinging is his mania to investigate and analyze. Instead of loving his partner, he analyzes him—and occasionally himself at the same time—and thereby cripples every fruitful relationship, dissecting and destroying what could be active life.

Aside from his ever present and frequently used stinger, another part of Scorpio's shadow side is his failure to recognize how little he actually sees the world about him objectively. Viewed from his psychic reality, he considers the world about him to be exploitative, hard, unsympathetic, ungrateful, immobile and dead, petite bourgeois, and consumed with superficial hedonism. He is not aware that he is battling the enemy—or the god—in himself. Scorpio seeks him "outside" and summons him by provoking his fellow man.

129

Very often Scorpio feels himself misunderstood, and he is right, for there are not many people who can—over the long haul—follow him completely into his heights and his depths.

Mars is not merely contained in Scorpio. Mars is the function, the power in human beings, that leads to the image of this sign of the zodiac—Scorpio.

If Scorpio succeeds in gaining insight into this nature and his potentialities, he can also understand others and accept the dark sides in them as in himself; then he can, for example, become a "wounded healer" (or an analyst).

The body zone assigned to Scorpio are the sexual organs. These organs, like the sexual act or sexuality in general, hold in an analogous symbol what is true for Scorpio and for Mars: in the realm of sexuality there is the polarity of Venus in Taurus and Mars in Scorpio, of earth and water, body and soul. It is a question of the conflict between asserting and satisfying self and sacrifice and devotion; a conflict between enticement, battle, and energy discharge; enjoyment and expansiveness; hurting and misusing; heights and depths; exulting to heaven or depressed to hell. It is a question of destruction, or new life, of becoming alive.

Sagittarius

Planet Jupiter
November 22—December 21

Following the two fundamentally opposed movements—in Libra where Venus assumes the function of mediation and in Scorpio where Mars is the force inciting commotion or working mortal terror, but through which new dynamics are evoked—the third sign of the quadrant again has the character of reconciling the opposites. But here it a question of more than mere synthesis. Sagittarius belongs to the element fire and brings in an entirely new impulse. The Sun's entrance into Sagittarius announces once again an entirely new aspect of the Sun symbol, now under Jupiter's leadership.

The darkest period of the year begins, with the longest nights and even gloomy days. (For psychotherapists, it is a time filled with work, because for all patients life is more difficult, especially for those who are psychically labile. Beginning already in Scorpio, it is a time of the greatest number of depressions.)

But the first hope of new light begins precisely in the deepest darkness. In the ecclesiastical year, Sagittarius's time is the period of Advent in which the arrival of the child, the light bringer, is awaited. We believe in and hope for something fundamentally new.

The image of Sagittarius was known in ancient Babylonian times. With the drawn bow and the double crown on his head, Sagittarius was regarded as the bearer of regal power (Boll, Gezold and Gundel 1977, part 2, appen.). Later the Egyptians and the Greeks adopted this symbol. Sagittarius has always been found in double form: as human and as animal, usually as a centaur with the body of a horse. But while the Greeks usually saw centaurs as violent and coarse, in this centaur they saw Chiron.

Sagittarius

Chiron was a son of Saturn.[25] He was friendly and wise. He knew the powers of places and their healing effects, and also of music, which he greatly loved. This linked him with Apollo, the "far-shooter," and from the latter Chiron acquired the gift of shooting the bow. Chiron became the teacher and mentor of Jason, Aesculapius the physician and his sons, of Achilles, and of others. As a son of Saturn, he was immortal, but he ceded this gift to Prometheus, who gave humankind fire (Sagittarius is, after all, a fire sign).

The planet belonging to this sign is Jupiter. We are reminded of Jupiter's victory following his battle with the Titans and cosmic powers, when he ultimately had to summon the Hecatonchires (the hundred-handed monsters) from the underworld to assist him in his final victory. In the sequence of signs of the zodiac, it is not a battle with Titans but rather a struggle between life and death which comes before the Sun reaches the sign Sagittarius and Jupiter's power to affect things. Here, too, Pluto's realms had opened alarmingly: abysmal things and threatening energies were liberated in Scorpio.

In the image of Sagittarius, we can see a combination and interpenetration of Scorpio and Libra: here animal strength (horse power) and the human form come together; the sureness of instinct, strength, and wise vision, a friendly heart, proportion, and harmony.

Likewise, the image of Sagittarius contains elements of the sign opposite it, Gemini, but exceeds Gemini by far. There the two aspects were divided between two brothers, one muscular and the other a music-loving figure. Both first had to become acquainted with and stake out their own realms, building a wall around their city. Sagittarius unites the various aspects into one figure and can now again burst the boundaries. Sagittarius's goal lies in the distance, "in the stars." Sagittarius aims for infinity, for new realms.

Three domains are united in the image of Sagittarius: the animal, the human, and that which transcends humankind. The three domains distributed by Jupiter in the myth are here again united under his function: the bow of Sagittarius embraces heaven, earth, and its depths. A new psychic range has become possible: admission of opposites, their complementary union, and transcendence.

Each of these three realms—the instinctive drive nature, the human social life, or the religious ideal—can be lived by itself. Likewise, all can come together in one task, in one context. Movement on all planes is addressed in the sign Sagittarius. Joy in achievement and movement can distinguish Sagittarius just as can intellectual agility and openness. Broad or distant horizons can be sought in the outer world in travel and in large undertakings—and can be found in the inner world.

Not so long ago, hippies traveled to India; today the innermost concern has come closer to home yet still lies "in the stars": in the environment and its protection. The green movement has brought nature and the proper way to deal with it—such as Chiron practiced—back into focus again.

A new ordering of the world is again necessary, as it was in Jupiter's day. With Jupiter as the planet corresponding to Sagittarius, a new consciousness in humankind as well as new values can be generated and new possibilities created. Granted, for this to happen new goals must be targeted with newly harnessed energies. In between lie periods of exhaustion and disappointment; but also times of regeneration and newly accumulating strength. Thus, again and again in Sagittarius, hope and trust that new goals, values, and orders can be found and summoned into life arise.

The various goals reflect the differing levels of Sagittarius qualities. From these also arise the shadow aspects that consciousness does not perceive. Sagittarius is always in motion. The less he can unite the various realms and yet actualize them as autonomous possibilities, the more he will preach them. The less comprehensive his own experience of life is, the more threadbare and fanatical will be his missionary zeal. He confuses the goal for which he strives and his own person. Thus one can meet the shadow of the educator in the moralist and that of the helper in the do-gooder who loves to pounce on victims, feeling compelled to help them. Other persons are led to the right path even if Sagittarius is not going somewhere. Misunderstood Sagittarius qualities appear in self-righteous moralism, in magnanimity that afterward keeps accounts or calculates the thanks. Or the actual inner goal can be missed due to haughtiness and pretentiousness.

The body area assigned to Sagittarius are the hips. This image, too, has its symbolic character.

Anatomically, the hips link the lower limbs with the trunk, the hip joints being the joints between the thigh and the pelvic bone. The pelvis comes together in front in the pubis and articulates behind with the sacrum, upon which the lumbar, thoracic, and cervical vertebrae rest, i.e., the spinal column that carries the head and supports the body.

The hips are the boundary between "below" and "above." They make possible the upright human posture. We must be able to move the hips freely if we are to assume a "correct" stance. Only then do we stand firmly on the ground and move—from the hips—without bracing ourselves. In this stance, the image of the human being is an image of the union of heaven and earth, just like the image of Sagittarius.

The difficulty, in the inner as in the outer world, in finding the "right" stance—which develops so naturally in the child—is shown by adults' frequent lumbar difficulties or by a great variety of pains that come about through incorrect posture. But the posture is determined by the meaning that Sagittarius sees before or within— and by the extent to which he or she can realize or actualize it.

Capricorn

Planet Saturn
December 22—January 19

With Sagittarius and Jupiter, new horizons appeared. They were concerned with those things essential to humankind, with transpersonal goals, with humankind's meaning.

133

With Capricorn, a new, final quadrant begins. Now a response is demanded to everything perceived: the realization, the concrete actualization. The Sun enters the sign Capricorn on December 22. That is the lowest point on its course: the winter solstice.

Capricorn, again a cardinal sign, stands in the sign of the return of the light. At this time, the birth of the child is celebrated in Christianity, the child who, as the Christ, is to be the Light of the World. From the depths begins the ascent into the heights, out of obscurity (the stable and the manger) something new emerges into the light and into the world.

The element assigned to Capricorn is earth: matter, concrete reality. In the gospel according to Matthew, it is said of Jesus: "The Word became flesh." The "word" of God incarnated has "materialized" and become "true God and true Man." This realization is praised in the old Christmas carols and new hope arises.

But even where the Christian symbols are no longer alive, people have similar experiences. Even in the most profane passage of the days between Christmas and Epiphany (January 6), remnants of the old forms of experiencing and acting are preserved. They reveal the need to look back over the past year and to get a view of the new. We make New Year's resolutions, we get a bank statement and start figuring our taxes for the year past. It is a time of endings and new beginnings.

Capricorn is a mountain goat. He lives in the high mountains, seeks out lonely regions far from human habitation, withdraws far above the permanent snowline. He prefers to live in sparse forests, on mountain slopes and gravelly precipices, on barren cliffs and crags. Mountain goats love companionship of their own kind but are cautious and shy toward other animals. They are tremendously skilled climbers and jumpers and run surefootedly over the most dangerous places. Even a slight unevenness on the face of a cliff is enough for them to get a footing and climb higher. The mountain goat has great strength and endurance, needs little food, and makes do with even the sparsest stands of grass. Already during the first month of life, the mountain goat's horns begin to emerge. Breeding time is in January, "the time of the mountain goat." Old goats often live as hermits; but inherent in all is the urge toward the heights.

In almost all cultures, the symbol of virility is linked with that of the goat. In the zodiac, the sign of the mountain goat

(Capricorn) stands in the phase of the return of the light; that of the ram (Aries) in the final victory of the light.

The planet Saturn belongs to the zodiacal sign Capricorn. Here it is a question of actualizing values that have been recognized, which always demands effort, work, and discipline. Saturn gives this empowerment.

"When the time had been fulfilled" it was not Olympian abundance but Saturnine parsimony that governed at the birth of the divine child; not radiance but the darkness of the stable and the absence of outer safety and protection. Similarly, Zeus grew up at first in concealment, hidden in a cave and fed on goats' milk before he finally could approach the light.

The path out of darkness toward the light demands the individual's continuing work. Qualities revealed by the image of Capricorn, which also belong to Saturn, help in this: strength, endurance, moderation, tenacity, and perseverance; the ability to take on hard conditions as a challenge, just as Saturn turned stony ground into arable land.

These characteristics depicted in Capricorn's nature are psychic qualities that arise from the "inner zodiac." Depending on individual endowment, one Capricorn is fascinated more by the frugality and endurance of this animal, another more by its striving for the heights where others can barely live; yet another is shaped by the daring art of climbing and leaping, be it to enjoy the solitude or an extensive vista and broad horizon.

Specifically, this can mean flexible perseverance and resilience in the battle of life, toughness, inflexibility, the ability to get one's way; the capacity to overcome obstacles of all sorts through tireless pursuit of a goal once set. Capricorn must translate his intention into action, not because he wills it (which would be Leo's way), but because it has to be that way.

It is important to Capricorn to serve a task, but also to master it, and perhaps also his colleagues. Capricorn is concerned with satisfying his urge to be effective, with self-respect, but also with public acknowledgment when he has achieved something on his own. Climbing the career ladder may lure him, the desire to be visible from afar, to lay himself open to criticism. On the other hand, obligations and the need to be effective are also a burden for Capricorn that nevertheless prod him on to further accomplishments.

For all of this, Capricorn's feeling life remains "a private affair," that is, he is able to grant it only a little space. Or he has to conceal it from himself as though he feared his antipode, the

135

sensibility and responsiveness to feelings of Cancer and Cancer's sensitivity and vulnerability. In a double sense, Cancer is for him a warning example: he shows Capricorn completely different possibilities for living, but also the endangerment that arises from them. In his behavior toward his fellows, Capricorn will be correct, but above all he will preserve his emotional independence and do this in consequence of a practical commandment; this way he does not feel himself emotionally obligated to anybody. Concrete obligations, explicit contracts, however, are not something he avoids.

We begin to see how many nuances the Capricorn nature can assume: ambition and drive to accomplish; strivings for independence and freedom from obligations; thoroughness and perfec-

Capricornus. tionism; dignity and the feeling of self-worth as well as a power drive. Shadow aspects appear again: if a natural ambition is suppressed, if it is not acknowledged as a need or if it must be concealed from others, this trait then leads a shadow existence and finds expression increasingly in a negative way. Then we can always clearly recognize characteristics of "the old Saturn" from the time before he was deposed by Jupiter: moral narrowness, ambition, power lust, and fear of competition, of feelings, and of his own progeny start to appear. The consequences of this are isolation and rigidity. Capricorn then mistakenly believes he discovers these characteristics in others and combats them there, as long as his own shadow remains in the dark.

The bodily zone assigned to Capricorn are the knees. The further we follow the signs of the zodiac through the course of the year, the lower the anatomical reference point. The fact that the knees are assigned to Capricorn corresponds especially well to a symbolic interpretation of the interrelationship between the psychic content of the sign of the zodiac and its traditionally stated anatomical correspondence. For this reason, I will trace the relationship between Capricorn and the knee, symbolically understood, in somewhat greater detail.

The knee as an anatomical and physiological structure calls up two opposite associations in our understanding of the possibilities of human movement, both in the bodily and in an extended sense: we can either step forward boldly and get going, or we can bend our knee, kneel down, i.e., express submission or meekness.

The sign Capricorn begins with the winter solstice and the

"birth" of the light, of the divine child. But in the history of Christianity, this turned into a vexation: instead of a god or a king, Jesus entered the world as a servant.

To bow, kneel, serve—these are words that have a negative connotation in our times. They belong to an "old morality," to a discredited patriarchate or to a spirit of unfreedom. Only in conjunction with honor and dignity does one still "serve," for example, serving a great cause or, of necessity, in the military. Otherwise we "do" our tasks and "do" our various duties. In German, the word *knien*, to kneel, has also experienced a revaluation. If someone says that a person "kneels into something or into a task," this now sounds rather dogged and all too zealous. But a remnant of the original meaning of serving is still preserved, as when one fully dedicates oneself to a task, serves it "wholeheartedly," of when one "kneels into something" so that one becomes one with the task or the topic.

There always has been a positive attitude toward serving, inside as well as outside the Christian faith. An example of this is the saturnalia that was celebrated in Rome in Saturn's honor at the time of the winter solstice (in the sign Capricorn). During this festival, all hierarchical relationships were canceled out. Slaves were free for the duration of the festival; they also sat at the feast table and were served by their masters. This pointed toward the underlying meaning that masters as well as slaves belonged to a higher "master" or served a higher purpose and meaning.

In Capricorn's striving, we saw a striving for the heights. We saw inflexibility and toughness because usually we experience striving for the heights in this way. He loves the heights. Voluntarily he seeks them and obviously does not experience the hard life up there as hard, nor does he have any "ambition" to live up there. To him, the grasses are not sparse. He is in harmony with inner and outer worlds, with inner needs and with his way of life.

Aquarius

Planets Saturn and Uranus
January 20—February 19

When the Sun enters Aquarius on January 20, we in the northern hemisphere have reached the depths of winter. In nature everything is numb and rigid. In many places water has frozen to ice. Whatever is going to grow is still veiled. Now activities take place in the interior spaces, in social life, and in an extended sense also in the life of the soul. The time that, outwardly, offers the least variety calls forth an especially intense inner life.

Aquarius is a fixed sign. What was begun under the sign Capricorn can now become the sole theme. Now it is a question of an overview of the situation, of seeing all together the various possibilities of life and of passing on to others the knowledge gained.

The element assigned to Aquarius is air. What presented itself as the task of the future must now be further worked out intellectually. The psychic functions assigned to this sign are Saturn and Uranus.

The constellation of this segment of the ecliptic is the water bearer: a human figure with a container in his hands that he holds at an angle out of which water pours. This image is like a summary of all the previously experienced Sun aspects in the various signs, of all possible experiences that have come to consciousness. The human being has now attained full erect stature. He has collected in himself, or in his earthen vessel, an abundance of experiences, insights, and knowledge and is now in the process of tipping this container so as to pass on, to pour out, what he has, and thus again to effect something new.

In the constellation, it is difficult to recognize the human form and the vessel. However, it is easy to see the flood of equally bright stars that represent the stream of water. That this image is not concerned with water, or with the wet element in the concrete sense, is shown by the assignment of this sign to the element air. Here it is intellectual contents that are intended and are "being poured out" (corresponding to this, the scorpion, living in hot and dry regions, belonged to the element water and thus to the emotional domain).

Whatever intellectual or psychic contents have collected in Aquarius's vessel exceed personal value or individual strength— values that were important in the opposite sign, Leo. Here are united collective values of consciousness that have proven themselves anew or experienced a revision in the experience of the individual and contents of the collective unconscious that the individual has experienced and raised to consciousness and that can now be handed on or disseminate.

In Aquarius, Saturnine endurance, conscientiousness, and the ability to digest and process have joined with creative ideas or impulses of Uranian diversity and penetrating power. There is the compulsion to pass on to others: The children of Uranus can no longer be left in caves and earthen containers. They must be seen and handed on; otherwise they will autonomously burst the bonds of fearful constriction.

In the psychic realm—corresponding to the inner zodiac—this is experienced as the urge for breadth, openness, and independence, for inner and outer freedom. Freedom of thought and for disseminating that thought are inalienable Aquarian traits. Aquarius relates them philosophically as well as psychologically. With Uranian impetus, this can lead to fundamental insights and, in other contexts, to technical inventions that often give rise to far-reaching developments.

Recognizing and anticipating interconnections, and hazarding visions of the future are Aquarian themes. Here, the exchange with others is important: among friends, in groups, in the team. Essential shared concerns can lead to the feeling of deep, comradely ties. Knowledge of spiritual and intellectual independence leads people with marked Aquarian qualities to a strongly pronounced individuality and to an intellectual pride that convinces others.

Here, there is a correspondence to the opposite pole: while the realm of personal power—being respected by the surrounding world—is emphasized in Leo, the emphasis in Aquarius is on spiritual and intellectual independence and freedom (and self-will). Hence, the danger arises that concrete life with its conditions will be neglected or experienced as exorbitantly demanding, for spiritual and intellectual freedom easily carries with it an uncompromising attitude toward practical life.

Various shadow aspects result from this. In interpersonal contact, the Aquarian is indeed always ready to give but does not find it easy to take, especially when it is a question of practical things, personal attention, or assistance. The exchange of giving and taking is possible in the spiritual and intellectual realm, and even there the Aquarian prefers to be the giver. Occasionally, this leads to a kind of eccentricity and to a lack of the humility that is a part of giving. The Aquarian can easily get into a certain innate withdrawnness from the practical aspects of life. Thus, he or she is often a poor judge of people. If he himself is noble, big-hearted, and open-minded, he also sees these possibilities in every one of his fellows. To the Aquarian, a beautiful face can only belong to a beautiful spirit. He is uncritical because reality interests him less than the world of his ideas. He projects his ideas of the good and the noble, or of the evil and the base, all the more easily the less he perceives the reality of the projection carrier.

Deficient reality sense can go so far (and here the shadow side leaps to the eye) that the Aquarian can wear two different socks without noticing it. At a restaurant, he cannot find his own overcoat because he never looked at it closely. Or he leaves the restaurant wearing another overcoat until he notices that the keys in the pocket do not work in his car. A person with pronounced Aquarian qualities will be little concerned with what the neighbors think, likewise, whether or not he perhaps disturbs them. He can produce the effect of being unpredictable or genial, and in fact can be both.

The Aquarian experiences difficulty linking saturnine demands in the element air (where they cannot be tackled "materially") and Uranian impulses. In the myth, they are overcome, "mastered," or castrated. Now it is a question of spiritual and intellectual mastery or psychic working through of stimulating and sometimes unsettling events and experiences. From this, the compulsion can arise (Saturn) to withdraw into the world of thought and ideas, to create a private world in the "airy" reaches and thus safeguard oneself against unpleasant realities. A pressing need may arise to plan the future precisely, to overplan it in order to preempt undesirable surprises by Uranus.

If Saturn is more strongly emphasized, acts of willfulness intended as security measures will be forced. If Uranus is emphasized, which can occur due to the *Zeitgeist*, it can come to the point of destructive impulses, revolts, or intuitions that can save the world. Saturn will seek either to subdue Uranus or to help him along the way to a "new age" when the two planets are in close proximity.

Compulsively forced intuitions find expression in the personal realm in deliberate individuality, in characteristics and behaviors expressed to the extreme, and in the pursuit of ruthless willfulness. Genuine independence of real, practical limitations in life, what in the good sense can be detachment, can in the negative sense turn out to be indifference, both toward oneself and one's own well being and that of others; one either ignores them or inundates them with one's own ideas and concerns. In both instances, there is a failure to imagine how the other person feels, the perception that he doesn't really exist as a real counterpart with his own structures of experience and feelings.

Indifference can also manifest in seeming magnanimity. Wrongly understood openness or freedom of values spare one emotional engagement, relieve one above all of experiencing deep feelings that could entail the loss of one's autonomy. The Aquarian is more interested in a committed word and a committed act, for he loves to turn things on their head, to ask unsettling questions and thereby provocatively wake others up.

The Aquarian is not concerned about inner equilibrium, as is the Libra, also in the same element. He cannot be thrown off balance because he does not seek it. He does not evade feelings because they burden him but rather because they bind him and could cost him his freedom. For the same reason, he can accept help only with difficulty and love only in moderation. If a beloved person gets too close, the Aquarian could feel his freedom restricted.

Experienced positively, Aquarius is an image of the mediator between various worlds and times. Where Capricorn ascended into the heights, Aquarius pours out the known and the proven into the depths. Aquarius is a font of "living water," of spiritual and intellectual life. We could view him as John the Baptist: unconcerned by his outer appearance and effects, he lets his call resound. He awakens us, he challenges us to turn back and to rethink, he inspires the heart to new ideas that could bring about a change in course vital for the future.

In reference to the body, Aquarius is assigned to the lower leg: the tibia, the fibula, and the ankle joint that articulates with the foot. The muscles surrounding the tibia and fibula along with the ankle joint enable the human being to walk with a resilient, springy step, the expression of the tension between Uranian intensity and Saturnine power.

In the image of the lower leg, two possible Aquarian attitudes are depicted: taking off from the Earth or turning toward Earth and her depths. The ability to separate from the Earth at a bound is a lethal temptation. In this connection, Adler (1950) and Riemann (1977) remind us of Antaeus: he was invincible as long as he remained in contact with the Earth, but when he leapt up, Hercules could slay him.

Without contact with the Earth that carries us, we are "out of touch," at times "flying high," and run the danger of neglecting our task or our meaning. Fortunately, we can bound away from the Earth only for short periods of time. This truly brings home to us that we are earthbound, and hence our task is to direct our spiritual and intellectual

Aquarius.

strength to the future of the Earth and toward the preservation of our Earth-given possibilities.

The sign of Aquarius holds a challenge: to garner so much practical experience that we can pour it as streams of living water are poured into the depths and benefit them.

Pisces

Planets Jupiter and Neptune
February 20—March 20

The zodiacal sign Pisces, the fishes, which the Sun enters on February 20, is the last segment of the ecliptic. After this 30° segment, the Sun again returns to the vernal point.

In our latitudes, the ice and snow melt; all that is hard yields to the soft element. The element water belongs to the sign Pisces. The last sign of this quadrant again has a dissolving or binding character. It dissolves the tension that could arise from the strivings in Capricorn and forms a countercurrent to the strongly emphasized Aquarian independence and uniqueness of individuality and originality that could drive a person into isolation.

The constellation Pisces is very long and drawn out, contains no large stars, and for the unskilled eye is practically impossible to find although in late summer (when the Sun is in the opposite sign, Virgo) Pisces does rise above the horizon.

The sign shows two fish with their backs to each other and yet linked together as though with a cord or band. In other representations, it is a pair of fish that stand side by side, head to tail. This pair cannot see each other, in any case not "eye to eye"; they cannot consciously recognize each other.

As two fish they are like the twin brothers, but unlike them not bound together in a unity as two aspects of one essence that is being challenged to discover and demarcate their particular domain. The fish are two as if to emphasize that here there is no question of the individual. The constellation of the two fish is also spread out so widely that we can hardly take it in at one glance.

In the occidental interpretation of the sign of the fish, Pisces, a great role has always been played by the reference to

Christ, whose symbol or secret sign was the fish.[26]

The two planets assigned to the sign Pisces are Jupiter and Neptune. First we will follow them in their domains and the fishes in their element, water.

With Jupiter, a new world order, a separation and distribution of the realms as well as life on different planes became possible. This ordering of life meets our striving for consciousness halfway, so that with the Jupiter aspects we are to some extent ready to familiarize ourselves with the world.

In the psychological context, Neptune's realm corresponds to the unconscious; it is still so new to occidental consciousness that people shy away from coming to terms with it. Consequently, our knowledge of Neptune's realm is extraordinarily meager. As an analogy to this, we may consider how little most people know about the life forms that live underwater.

Fish are vertebrates, as are humans. But few of us know anything about the more than 25,000 species that have existed for 450 million years in the sweet and salt waters of the Earth and that lay between two and ten million eggs per year. Fish have distinct senses of sight, hearing, smell, and taste. Moreover, they also have a kinesthetic sense that permits them to register the movements of current and tremors over very great distances. They are predators, eating not only insects, worms, and vegetation, but also other fish, which sometimes can be much larger than they are themselves. The size of fishes varies from about a quarter of an inch to 50 feet.

Neptune's realm exceeds by far our capacity to imagine it. Here, variety rules, a life in the depths that is just as incomprehensible to us as is the starry sky above. And since we see into the depths even less than into the heights above, we can raise the treasures of this living world into our consciousness only with difficulty.

Thus, it is not to be understood only in a metaphorical sense when we read in Jung—or in any other depth psychological formulation—that fish represent contents of the unconscious. The unconscious is the collective source ground out of which we all live and which will continue to exist when our personal, inner sun has set, when our ego consciousness has died. The fullness of the collective unconscious will not diminish even when additional contents are elevated out of it into the light, into collective consciousness, since they regenerate themselves out of themselves, like life in the deep waters.

In the ancient religions, fish are symbols both of death and fertility, like the sea itself. In the Old Testament, Jonah experienced the nearness of death when he was devoured by a fish, and new birth when the fish later cast him onto land again. According to Hindu belief, a fish saved Manu, the ancestor of humankind, from the deluge. In India, fish have been recognized since early times as signs of good luck and fertility.

In the sign of Sagittarius, the planet Jupiter's question was of fruitful new orientation, a distant goal, and the correct attitude toward it. Whence could that come if not out of the creative depths of which we are still unconscious, and whither might we aim if not into regions that transcend our consciousness? This is the context and sense in which we can regard the zodiacal sign Pisces, fishes, as determined by Jupiter's and Neptune's shaping powers.

Viewed psychically, persons who are strongly shaped by this sign of the zodiac will always experience a tension between meaningful devotion (Jupiter) and a losing of self, a surrender of self (Neptune), followed by the feeling of not having a sufficiently strong "I." Speaking figuratively, these two sides always turn their backs to each other, cannot consciously look each other in the eye, and consequently cannot join together. Always there is first the one feeling, then the other, as the basic experience: joy in empathic surrender and devotion and the feeling of being submerged in anonymity and the feeling of being worthless.

A great adaptive capacity is inherent in the Piscean nature (corresponding to fish in the sea, which take on the color of their surroundings). They themselves, as well as the people around them, may often experience this as agreeable, but at other times experience it as a lack of character. Fish—Pisceans—are easily washed away. Every large wave carries them with it for a distance before they even perceive it. This can transpire in all human relationships, especially in the area of sex. After having swum with the current and resonated with the dominant chord, Pisceans sober up and have the feeling they have been used.

The search for security arises from the feeling of being exposed and without protection: the Piscean senses a great need for moral support or would like to dissolve in a relationship. This may place excessive demands on the partner, indeed he or she may feel exploited, for the partner also wants a life of his or her own and not only to be a supplier of protection. Where security cannot be found in a partnership, it is sought in groups and communities. This can offer aid and relief, but it also promotes the Piscean's lack of independence. Uncommon sensitivity and permeability is part of the nature of Pisces; we need think only of the fish's sensorium for tremors and currents that registers every movement of the waves. Pisceans feel with and suffer with others, so very much so that they also suffer the inability to defend themselves against it. Hence, there are two possibilities: either to join in, to affirm this talent, to live it, and to arrive at spiritual and intellectual depths, or to evade it anxiously, to protect oneself, to relinquish all responsibilities, to delegate activities and decisions, to disappear into the family or the community and be perpetually, self-sacrificingly active.[27] But for the environment, this is not only good fortune but also a burden and the continual demand for some form of attention and gratitude.

Here the shadow aspects of Pisces begin to appear when a lack of sense of self is taken to be self-sacrifice. The hope or demand is that others provide security, and it is ultimately attained in a sort of gentle rape (fish can devour their own kind, sometimes even those larger than themselves). At the human level, this may mean: "I love you so much I could eat you!" A deficient point of view or personal stance is given out as tolerance. The need for symbiosis is called love; one believes one is a partner and remains a dependent child. The childish wish for security, for being spoiled and taken care of arises out of helplessness. When disappointments come and hopes are not fulfilled, there quickly arises the impression that one has been handed over to the wickedness of the world. Other Pisceans "endure" this "mean world" and cultivate their suffering in it so much that they ultimately misunderstand their capacity for suffering as strength. This supposed strength can even be mixed with harshness and a withholding attitude—as self protection.

Unfortunately, the Piscean soul is not happy even then, because it is not living in accordance with its inner pattern.

In the realm of the body, the feet are appointed to the sign of Pisces. This may seem surprising, because the fish is distinguished precisely because it has no feet. But, once again, how marvelously fitting and comprehensive is this symbol.

Today, it is again being widely recognized that every part of the body can be reached and beneficially influenced through the feet. Each part of the body—be it stomach, heart, head, shoulder, intestine, etc.—corresponds to some part of the foot, to each reflex zone.[28] Hence the sensitivity and permeability with which Pisceans are burdened is also their great gift: in the most subtle ways, they can understand other persons, feel their way into them, and have a healing effect on them.

Through the feet, each person participates in the quality of the zodiacal sign Pisces. If we could succeed in becoming more conscious of them and of standing on the Earth in the right way, we would have fulfilled a part of the meaning of our being on Earth, be this in Jupiter's sense or in the sense of the Christ whose sign was *ichths*.

If "standing on one's own feet" means independence and steadfastness, then Pisceans have a very hard time of it precisely because fish have no feet. But if they can plunge into their element, into the realm of empathy and resonating with others, if they can become absorbed in greater tasks or higher goals, they are as alive as "a fish in water."

In conclusion, I want briefly to confront an extremely common misunderstanding that leads to the protest: "I found myself in my sign" or "I can't recognize my colleague, for example, in Taurus."

Today, it has become a habit to overvalue the position of the Sun in a one-dimensional way. Again and again, we hear "X is a Taurus," "Y is a Virgo," which takes into account only the position of the Sun. Now without a doubt the position of the Sun can be of great significance for prominent characteristics of a person. But it is equally possible that those personality characteristics that are easily discernible in an individual have been shaped only in small measure by the Sun's position because other, more dynamic, more significant constellations between planets and signs of the zodiac can be sensed more distinctly. Likewise, the house in which the Sun is located (see the next part) is decisive, that is, it is the area of life in which the individual's ego consciousness, will, and self-reliance can find their principal expression.

For example, a Leo may not exert a "leonine" effect, but rather, although he remains a Leo, in his externally visible manifestation is more intensely informed by other, more striking relationships, at least at first glance.

III

The Houses

Houses, Zodiac, and Planets
Title page woodcut by Erhard Schön in
Leonhard Reymann, Nativity Calendar (1515)

The position of the planets in the signs of the zodiac is approximately the same for all persons born on the same day. The uniqueness of the individual horoscope arises only when we take into account the place and moment of birth—when we calculate the houses. Only when we consider the place and precise time of birth can we reconstruct which sign of the zodiac was rising over the horizon in the east at the time of birth (the so-called "ascendant"), and likewise which was descending below the horizon in the west (the "descendant"). Similarly, we can now establish what sign stood at the zenith (the "midheaven" or *medium coeli*) and correspondingly which was concealed at the opposite pole, at the nadir (the *immum coeli*).

If by chance someone is born on March 21, the equinox, at 6 a.m. at 0° longitude, that person's Sun is located precisely on the axis of the horizon, and the rising sign, the ascendant, is 0° Aries. At midday, the Sun stands in the zenith at 0° Capricorn; at 6 p.m., it sets at 0° Libra; and at midnight, it is in the nadir at 0° Cancer.

There is a cross formed of the east-west and zenith-nadir axes, which subdivides the zodiac into four sections, the four quadrants. This left-right, above-below axial cross corresponds to an inner structure in the human being. Likewise, it corresponds to what Kepler called our "geometric instinct" to further subdivide

149

each of these quadrants into three "fields" or "houses" and thus again arrive at the number twelve which we experience in the zodiac.[29] The houses refer to individual locations and are not of equal size, as are each of the 30° signs of the zodiac, a situation due to the slanted position of the ecliptic in regard to the horizon and to the celestial equator. The houses can vary in their size and are not congruent with the signs of the zodiac. This results in the multiplicity of individual variants, even leaving out of account the differing positions of the planets and their aspects to one another.

The twelve houses do not reflect "heavenly" or "divine" realities as do the signs and the planets, but rather "earthly realities." They represent twelve areas of life in which the person should actualize the planetary energies in the sense of the related zodiacal sign. Each house deals with a specific theme, and each theme must be lived concretely.

Division into houses was known in Babylon and Egypt. Originally, it was not always twelve, just as the signs of the zodiac had not been established as twelve. The names of the houses varied, as we can well imagine, from time to time and culture to culture, for the "areas of life" changed as did times and cultures.

Yet essentially, the houses have remained the same, for they correspond to basic patterns of human life tasks. What is innate in a human being and what he encounters in life or what he himself brings about becomes a theme in the houses. The basic endowment is the same in all persons, for all of us partake of the primordial psychic ground, the collective unconscious, which contains the basic patterns of all the possible human experiences. On the other hand, the manner in which the aspects of human existence are lived varies greatly depending on which archetypes are constellated in relation to each other in the individual and what external conditions for actualization exist.

To this extent, the signs of the zodiac and the planets can be called collective symbols; however, the individual horoscope is an individual symbol. It indicates the particular themes pertaining to the individual and the constraints under which he can fulfill his tasks and actualize his goals.

It is not surprising that the themes of the houses correspond to those of the signs of the zodiac, for the psyche—in accordance with its structure—"recognized" the latter in the outer world of the stars. The signs of the zodiac mirror the Sun in the course of the year, and the houses indicate the themes of the course of life, or of the various areas and stages of life. In the planets, we find the functions, the formative energies, that condition and shape us.

When we considered the signs of the zodiac, we saw that the dynamism commenced with the accentuation of the vernal point at the beginning of the zodiac at 0° Aries through imbalance. Again and again, we confirm that one movement elicits a countermovement and thereby causes a further progression. Thus, in the horoscope the ascendant, the beginning of the first house, places the first strong accent. The remaining houses follow in counterclockwise direction like the signs of the zodiac. The meaning of the houses also corresponds to the content of the signs in their sequence starting at the vernal point: the first house always has an Aries quality, even if it is defined in the individual case by another sign of the zodiac. The second house has a Taurus character; the third is defined by Gemini; etc.

I will preface the following discussion by presenting the names of the houses that have been used for centuries. As absurd as they may sound, we are able to see in the course of a closer examination that they have always contained the same essential content. But the interpretation depends on the context in which we comprehend them. Then, in what follows, I adopt as the modern terms those concepts that Ring (1956–1973) uses to characterize the houses.

First House

Old Designation: Vita *(Life)*
New Designation: Personality

The moment of the vernal point, when the Sun crosses the celestial equator, corresponds to the moment of birth, the cutting of the cord, when the baby utters its first cry and breathes for the first time. Only now does it have its own circulatory system and metabolism, having become an independently functioning organic being.

The ways in which newborns scream can vary greatly; likewise, the ways in which the environment reacts can vary. The way a human being looks into the world and experiences it subjectively and how his fellows react to him, how they encounter him, will also vary.

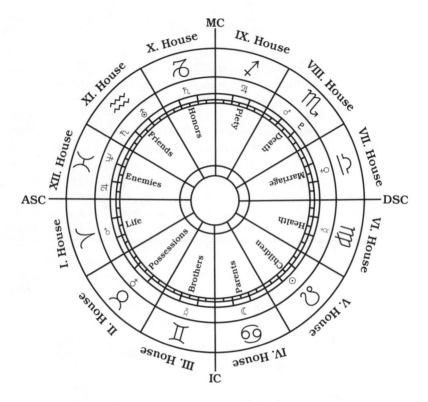

In the Middle Ages, the names of the houses were presented in two lines:

    Vita—lucrum—fratres—genitor—filii—valetudo
    nuptiae—mors—pietas—honores—amici—inimici

The ascendant corresponds to Aries leaping toward the
light. The ascendant indicates the needs that the individual instinctively senses, by which the individual is defined even before
he or she realizes them. They are like a skin which a person
wears and cannot shed. This skin can vary greatly depending on
the sign that informs the first house and may also proclaim itself
to others in a variety of ways. Others will then answer and respond in a corresponding variety of ways.

How differently the world is experienced—and how great
the variety in the world's response:

> When a young buck comes bounding along, or when a ram
> balks, gets out of line, leaps forward, acts bellicose.

Or when a fellow with a thick hide and broad shoulders stands there, waiting, taking his time, taking it easy, taking a long time to get ruffled.

Or when another approaches the world sympathetically, with interest and openness, obligingly, courteously, diplomatically.

Or, on the other hand, when one is reserved, agreeable but rather shy, timidly waiting to see if one is going to be hauled away, who must first overcome oneself before one can greet the neighbor.

Again another can stand there just so: "Here I am, isn't that marvelous?"

And then again another: courteous, obliging, but not too much; mildly reserved.

Surely this is how it is. Thus, briefly stated, the first six signs of the zodiac on the ascendant can present themselves as possibilities of how they determine the attitude toward the world.

Since the ascendant (as the first cardinal point or sector in the horoscope) strongly influences the entire "primary" nature of the individual, the planet working in this sign of the zodiac has been called the "birth ruler." We saw that the function that the planet represents in the sign cannot be separated from the sign itself. Now, likewise, it will be of particular significance or formative power for those whose ascendant (ASC) lies in this sign.

Further we can imagine that the first step into life, the "first appearance" or the fundamental attitude, can be generally decisive for the manner in which life will be experienced. There are always two aspects to this: first, the way I experience myself, others, and the surrounding; second, the way the surroundings experience me. This holds consequences for the entire life. *Vita*, life, therefore, is simply how the first house is designated.

Here we must keep in mind that a conscious ego develops only in the course of later childhood out of the child's original unconscious condition. Only after the ego has differentiated from the environment is it possible to make a conscious choice among various possibilities and to construct a persona (a mask).

We often speak of the mask, the persona attitude of the first house. But to do so is to misunderstand the concept C. G. Jung introduced or to misunderstand the first house. According to ancient astrological tradition, the first house represents the individual's initial situation, whereas, by definition, the persona refers to an achievement of the conscious ego as it comes to terms with the world around it.

The first house always has an Aries character. This means the quality of the first house is decisive for my variety of demands on myself and on the world, for the manner of initiative that I instinctively assume and that will shape the style in which I address myself to the various areas of life; and likewise for the stance I take toward the world and react to it.

(It goes without saying that the various signs of the zodiac in which the first house can be situated, and the various planets that may be found in the first house, will influence the basic qualities of the first house I have described here. Although it cannot be emphasized often enough, the same holds true for all the succeeding houses.)

Second House

Old Designation: Lucrum *(Riches, Profit)*
New Designation: Possessions

The second house is concerned with finding a secure foundation. It corresponds to the sign Taurus, the bull. Here the wish appears to get solid ground under one's feet, be it in the image of Venus stepping onto land or the image of the bull that grazes in his meadow or rests there and chews his cud. What rules here is the need for well-being, security, warmth, for meadows with abundant food. In the image of the bull, Taurus, all sorts of things are taken on one's shoulders—or accepted as part of the bargain. He grazes what he can, but he also chews his cud: he enjoys what he has taken in, even in double measure.

The nature of the "nourishment" or basis sought will vary depending on the sign of the zodiac that gives this house its opening tone: it may be concerned with physical well-being, material possessions; or equally with books or themes that are collected and cataloged; with art that one uses—and with all that one would possess, incorporate, and enjoy.[30] Even difficult themes (for example, as is the case with the Scorpio character) are not released but repeated, chewed over again.

This has to do with security, protection, assurance, with the vitally necessary basis in the material or also in the spiritual and intellectual domain (depending on the sign). It falls to the lot of one person with ease (with Jupiter's assistance); another must labor for it (with Saturnine endurance); yet another appears to be indifferent, if, for example in the Aquarian way, he thinks (or does not think) about the material foundation (in which case the basis for independence and inner as well as outer freedom will be that much more essential). The fundamental tendency in this house is to sate oneself with what one essentially needs for life and savor it to the full.

If there is no planet in this house, the theme of the necessary vital security will be sounded by the sign alone. Being "occupied" by one or more planets will clearly indicate the importance of the concern and the psychic as well as the external, concrete behavior, the possible ways of working with this theme.

Saturn in the second house does not have to signify poverty, labor, or avarice. Saturn can also cause one to be tough, persistent, able to bear up under burdens, and modest in achieving one's fundamental security. Mars does not have to imply pillaging but rather can also suggest initiative and an enterprising spirit, but certainly in an impulsive and forceful manner, as Mercury would act here, and so on.

In the second house, the native instinctively desires with a vital elan whatever will satisfy the basic needs. It takes time for something to grow and attain maturity. The bull is slow, and one must let both material as well as spiritual goods develop at their own speed.

Lucrum, riches, is what this house was named. Whether or not one is satisfied and in accord with his efforts and the possessions he has gained is the realm in which the feeling of being rich manifests. It is not the zeros after a number in a bank account that make one rich. It has to do with the subjective experience of being rich—or not, with satisfaction or with chasing after more, with avarice.

The spectrum of the second house extends from pure incorporation to the spiritual and intellectual enjoyment of perfect happiness.

Third House

Old Designation: Fratres *(Brothers, Siblings)*
New Designation: Developmental Path

Since ancient times the third house has been called "brothers" or "siblings." In the image of the sign of Gemini, we found twin brothers. The one pair (Castor and Pollux) differed in what they possessed: immortality and mortality. The other pair (the sons of Antiope) differed in what they were capable of and what, again, comprised their natures: manual dexterity and strength in the one, musical and poetic talents in the other, abilities with which not only to express themselves but also to have an effect on the world around them.

In the realm of the third house, we first take note of what actually are the possibilities of life. Exchange and mutual understanding are necessary. One must learn to see interconnections and, in general, learn a great deal in order to get through life. Love of exchange is necessary as well as the readiness to share with each other and to share oneself, just as the two sets of twins did.

As the mediator between the realms, between above and below, east and west, Mercury is at home in this house: the teacher of clever speech and language; of music, craft, and handling and processing of any subject and any matter. He can give assistance in finding one's own mode of expression and in recognizing and developing inherent possibilities. The beginnings of all exchange lie in the domain of the family and take place among siblings, for example. Relatives and short trips were also assigned to this house, both of which serve the purpose of becoming acquainted with the world. As always, this holds true for the concrete as well as for the psychic domains. The brothers and siblings can be concrete siblings or the other side in oneself. And it is both. If a boy has no brothers, he will the more readily feel himself compelled to discover brothers in playmates or even in figures of his fantasy.

In the domain of the third house, the surrounding world is taken in as though by breathing. One assimilates what suits one, what nourishes and refreshes "the blood," the river of life. And one eliminates, forgets what is not utilized. Thus it gradually becomes possible to find one's own modes of expression, one's own knowledge and a body of skills with which one imparts oneself to the surrounding world, communicates with it and cultivates one's interchange with it.

One's concerns will vary depending on the sign of the third

house: they can manifest on the concrete, material plane (determined by earth signs) or intellectually (air signs) or they can relate to emotional needs (water signs). They can also be guided by the impulsive drive for the possibility of expression (fire signs). Taking in can derive from an introverted attitude and likewise also correspond to an extraverted need for expression. In addition to the signs, of course, the planets that may stand in this house also determine the dynamic.

The third house is concerned with elementary communication, not communication with distant realms or partners, but communication in the vicinity, which explains the old designation "brothers, siblings." It is not totally "other" persons or distant parts of the outer world that must be included in the communication; rather, for the present, it is a question of coming to terms with what lies close at hand—and sometimes this means dealing with qualities within the individual.

Fourth House

Old Designation: Genitor *(Parents, Creator)*
New Designation: Source, Background

As the fourth house begins, we reach the next cardinal point, the "bottom of the sky," the *immum coeli* (IC). This house corresponds to Cancer and to the Moon function.

The fourth house can be viewed as the house of origins, the house of the parents, both temporally and in terms of psychological development, and as an emotional starting point, the influence of which continues from childhood until death.

The bottom of "my" sky contains my relationship to my origins, my inheritance, to the shaping experiences of the parental home, family (or substitute figures), ancestors, homeland, culture, etc. How did I experience the parents who shaped me? How did I experience the Moon principle? (In the chapter on the Moon, I discussed that here we are speaking of subjective experiences.) Was natural growth and maturation—represented by the various phases of the Moon—possible? Or were innate potentials buried in overzealous pedagogy, violations, or failures?

We always carry within us as our deepest foundation the impress and the essential forces of the fourth house (of its sign and of the planets found in it). Each night we return to the fourth house, the maternal womb, the unconscious. Here we experience regression and regeneration, a plunge into the world of dreams whose content, however, we can bring into the light, into consciousness.

The tendency of the fourth house is the search for support and security. If there are planetary powers here, they pull one back rather than toward an active life in the outer world. This "back" does not always signify back to the parents (at most, occasionally back to their financial or other support) but rather can also be a retreat into one's own inner world, the private sphere, one's own four walls. An appropriate image is that of the hermit crab. Shrinking back from the demands of the outer world can lure one into a game of hide-and-seek (even from oneself), be this in the studio, the bedroom, or sleep—or into any other suitable armor. This corresponds to the crab's backward movement when it encounters obstacles, which can come from the inner or the outer world. Similarly, the tendency to hold back corresponds to the pincers that do not let go of anything once taken hold of.

We know from experience how different parental homes can be, and we see it in the horoscope in the various signs, planets, and their aspects. We cannot succeed in laying aside or leaving behind the structures of the fourth house by a decisive act of will. In order to grow out of the source and be reintegrated into living processes, predispositions that are anchored must develop through maturation in keeping with the Moon principle.

What has shaped us and left its imprint is revealed in the fourth house. We cannot lay aside this inner image even if we have long since left our parents' home. "Parents" are more than the physical, bodily parents; in the *image* of mother and in the *image* of father, we experience what will determine our relationship to the male and female principles.

Fifth House

Old Designation: Filii *(Sons, Children)*
New Designation: Generativity

In the fifth house, we encounter impulses such as were contained in Leo and in the Sun. Here we are dealing with the need for spontaneous expression.

Filii—children—is what the fifth house used to be named. But before one can think of having children, one must first have been totally a child oneself. Many adults recall their own childhood with sadness that they never fully or adequately savored it. The child in them is not satisfied.

Part of being a child is the spontaneous expression, "I." How full of happiness and pride is the child when it can say "I." It savors this newfound sense of the world. Now, instead of speaking of itself in the third person—"Danny's coming"—it calls out: "I, I'm coming down stairs!" Leo possesses an intensified sense of self-worth, a sense of self-assurance that can be taken for granted, and this characterizes the quality of the fifth house.

In this house, for the adult, too, all those possibilities are contained that the child spontaneously lives. It expresses itself in movement, play, singing, and giving form. It is always open to new impulses and seizes them just as Leo's ever-watchful eye perceives everything and just as he knows how to realize his ideas.

Like the lion in his hunting ground, the child doesn't like to be disturbed. Usually a child defends himself quite as a matter of course (if it is not hindered by opposing signs and planets in this house, or by other influences in the fourth house). It simply gets its way, and only later does empathy or understanding for others awaken. These are well-known Leo qualities.

All inner life is translated into deeds, realized in some form. In the dynamism this contains, there also lies mastery of the world and validation of self. What the child lives spontaneously is what every person carries as a demand in himself or herself as the "inner" child. In our times, we are increasingly able to admit these inner needs. In the wake of exclusively rational thought, they were more or less suppressed and granted only to people such as artists, who in any case were relegated to settlements outside normal society.

But in the fifth house we are concerned not only with the "inner" child, just as in the second house it was not only a question of external possessions and in the third, not only an issue of concrete brothers. Fundamentally, *filii* refers to the relation to the child, to the real child, to one's own and to the children of others. Depending on the sign of this house (and whichever planets are also present in it), one's ways of being with children and their concerns are shaped.

At the symbolic level, the child also often signifies the future in that for the individual as for the collective it represents the continuation of life, i.e., the future. This symbol carries the future-oriented meaning of the fifth house in a very concrete sense: generativity, procreation. (The relationship to the future where the *spiritual* dimension is emphasized is carried by the eleventh house.)

Potential energy as well as energy being discharged belongs to the nature of Leo as well as the Sun. Aside from play and creative activity, we can experience this nowhere more impressively than in sexuality (which, of course, can also lead to children sometimes). Therefore it, too, has always belonged in the realm of the fifth house. The various nuances or variations in which we live it are again determined by the sign of the zodiac or the planets that are at work in the fifth house.

If the potentialities of this house are not made use of, or if planetary energies in it demand expression, there arises in the child as in the adult forms of distress. Unsatisfied hunger leads to substitute satisfactions. Letting other interests or occupations take the foreground so that one has no time or energy for the real themes of this house leads, in the course of time, to pronouncedly faulty behavior or experiencing, to inner sterility.

Filii, children, are the area of life in which the issue is to remain in contact with the creative, in touch with the child in us or with concrete children and their spontaneous power of expression.

Sixth House

Old Designation: Valetudo *(Health, Illness)*
New Designation: Work

One does not need very much life experience to notice that one's health, *valetudo*, as this house is called, is most intimately connected with the way one is accustomed to live one's life.

But the work one performs, be it in one's private or one's professional life, is also linked to the way one lives. Work has always been necessary merely to be able to eat and to clothe oneself. Thus, besides one's general life habits, work is most intimately associated with health. In many astrology books, the sixth house was called the house of work from the start, and health was added to it only later.

Part of the nature of Virgo, the sign that gives this house its character, is selecting and utilizing what is useful; constructing an overview; harvesting and processing. Here we are dealing with Mercurial qualities: efficacious action. Therefore, one must precisely assess and correctly engage the energies that are available.

One requirement of this sign is temperance: it is not private, personal interests that are cultivated here. It is the *task* that holds the foreground. The issue is concrete mastery of real commitments (in an earth sign). Mercury's workings make possible a rationalization of work in technical, physical, and psychic domains.

Best of all, Virgo likes very concrete tasks for which it is possible to have an overview. And Virgo can do in good faith only what corresponds to his or her personal uniqueness. For many people, it is simply part of their attitude toward work to identify themselves with it. It is the best basis for good accomplishments.

In relationships to other persons, Virgo is always rather reserved and cautious. This also offers a good basis for professional life, in regard to superiors, colleagues, or subordinates.

"Work is half of life," people used to say. Today the self-employed still say it: entrepreneurs or those in the helping professions, any work where one does not take advantage of the forty-hour week.

How differently this looks when one has the sixth house in Leo, perhaps also with the energies of the Sun and Venus; or if one has this house coinciding with Virgo, perhaps with Saturn and Mars.

In the long run, negative consequences for one's health cannot be avoided when there are excessive demands, compulsion to perfectionism, anxiety, emotional burdens, or psychic stress. When one enjoys pleasant working conditions and finds happiness in the meaning and success of one's work, one's health also is better. Yet we have seen it only superficially if we view the house of health as the house of work.

The sixth house is the last in the lower half of the horoscope. With each of the preceding houses, it has become increasingly clear that in each instance we have to be concerned with getting to know our own needs and innate potentials and the correct attitude toward them. Furthermore, there also is always the demand to become active, to translate knowledge, thoughts, and insights into deeds so that a healthy well-being becomes possible. In every house, it has been a question of creating harmony between the demands of the inner structures and those of the outer world. In the sign Virgo, it is also important to gain knowledge of what fully corresponds to one's personal uniqueness and to live accordingly. Here we must winnow the wheat from the chaff. From the vantage point of the end of the sixth house, we must cast a retrospective glance, we must examine the results: Have I been able to develop in accordance with my nature? Am I living healthily, whole? What is my worth?

If one is in harmony with oneself—as Virgo loves to be—this is the best foundation for health, of the body as well as of the soul.

Accordingly, when we look back over what we have said about the first six houses, we can see that these (lower) houses, as a whole, represent the more unconscious preconditions or given conditions for the individual.

But with perhaps greater justification, we could also say that the first half of the houses represents the individual's personality structure from a more introverted point of view.

But we have to consider this, too: depending on what signs of the zodiac appear in these houses and what planets are situated in this part of the horoscope, both the conscious–unconscious pair of opposites and the introversion–extraversion pair can undergo a different intermingling in any given horoscope.

Seventh House

Old Designation: Nuptiae *(Marriage, Extramarital Sex)*
New Designation: Cohabitation

A new quadrant begins with the seventh house. It is a cardinal house, an angular house (DSC), opposite the ascendant. It is defined by the sign of Libra and the function of Venus.

Here an entirely new theme is addressed. Now a "Thou" stands opposite the "I" that commenced its autonomous life at the ascendant. Where Mars demanded on the one side, Venus now answers on the other.

In older astrology, this was called *nuptiae*, which indeed does mean marriage but also extramarital sex. This points to the significance of the seventh house in astrology that here we are not

speaking only of the institution of marriage but of every sort of intense relationship, such as Venus and Mars expressly lived outside wedlock.

Depending on the emphasis exerted by planetary forces,
one is challenged to a variety of confrontations. And the shapes of
the concrete confrontation, the details of coming to terms, will differ depending on the sign that determines the seventh house.
That "I" and "Thou" challenge and condition one another always
remains the presupposition.

A real partner, man or woman, faces opposite one's own
emotional and physical needs, concretely. At the same time, however, so many expectations, hopes, and fears are projected onto
the other that he or she, and his or her true nature, are concealed, buried by these projections.

One always experiences the real partner in accordance
with one's own structures (almost independently of the way the
other really is). If Saturn is in Capricorn in one's own seventh
house, one experiences in one's partner a hard realist who limits
and constricts one. If Mars in Scorpio is in the seventh house,
then one feels, to put it simply, misused, overtaxed, and sucked
dry by one's partner.

On the other hand, one reacts correspondingly: in the first
case, one is cool, rejecting, setting limits that the partner must
observe. Or, in the other case, one is torn apart, stirred up, demands attention and a ready ear, and desires to be consoled.

Under friendlier or more propitious signs, the "Thou" can
perhaps be perceived more positively; but in any case it takes a
good deal of self-knowledge to be able to differentiate oneself from
the other, to withdraw projections, and as far as is possible to see
one's partner as a different sort of person. (But our perception always remains subjective.) Then more than a relationship or a
partnership is possible; marriage can still today be risked. Difficult constellations remain difficult, but we can better learn to do
justice to ourselves and to the other.

Did Venus love or let herself be loved? Did Venus chose or
let herself be chosen? Hers, Libra, is an air sign and a cardinal
sign. For Venus, there are no petty questions here but rather the
encounter of equally powerful forces that can hold each other in
equilibrium. In the element air, Venus is not rigid but relaxed,
cheerful, composed. She can judge interconnections—also within
a love relationship—and that means allowing them to become
conscious and bringing them into balance in that she sees both

sides, her own *and* that of the other person, her own part and what the concrete moment demands.

The scales of fate will show whether or not the heart, along with the mind and common sense, proves its worth in mastering the tasks of the seventh house.

Eighth House

Old Designation: Mors (Death)
New Designation: Life's Background

In the houses of the upper half of the horoscope, what has been achieved personally must now be tested and put to work in the service of further goals that transcend the individual: religious questions (ninth house), public influence (tenth), friends (eleventh), and enemies (twelfth) lie before us. We can view the twelve houses in the total context of a life process, and each area can become a primary concern in its own time.

To the eighth house are assigned Mars and Pluto in Scorpio. In addition to Saturn, we will also encounter Uranus in Aquarius in the eleventh house, and in the twelfth Neptune in Pisces, as well as Jupiter. Recently many astrologers have been leaving out Saturn and Jupiter in these signs. I consider this a misunderstanding. Mars, Saturn, and Jupiter can be experienced in a person's life in a more concrete manner. Uranus, Neptune, and Pluto, however, are so far distant from us and remain so long in a sign (Pluto, for example, for more than twenty years), that they are experienced more in connection with general trends of the age, with the *Zeitgeist*, or with collective movements by which every individual is, of course, also affected.

We saw that in the sign of Scorpio a battle between life and death was played out. Since ancient times, the eighth house has been regarded as the house of death, in the literal and the extended sense. Life also means perpetual death, continually having to surrender. (The image of the life process as a constant descent after the ascent to life's midpoint is only a pale image for this.) Yet we sometimes see "*Una ex his*" on clocks, which means "One of these [hours will be your last]." This does not mean one should be anxious about one's life, but rather one should live correctly. Give yourself fully to this hour—it could be your last. Use it sensibly.

Only complete surrender, "being completely carried away redeems the guilt of earth" (Borchardt 1957, p. 277).

When we considered the sign Scorpio, we saw that the feeling of being carried away is not always sweet but carries within itself a bitter thorn. Whoever comes into contact with the night side of life (the scorpion is an animal active at night) is catapulted to the heights as well as plunged into the depths, and loses all sense of security.

Here we hear the challenge: How secure is my foundation? Will I be carried? Will I get through it when my soul challenges me to battle? When it becomes a question of transformation? When I open myself fully to the mortal play of life and death? Am I ready to surrender security for the sake of greater depths, for processes of the soul's development?

This has always been a theme of for young people when they renounce possessions and security, perhaps also when they take drugs to intensify their emotional experiences. Whether or not the foundation in fact will hold differs from case to case.

The battle between the second and the eighth houses is well fought if one succeeds in crying out, as did Jacob when he fought with the angel, "I will not release you lest you bless me!" (That battle took place before Jacob was able to bring home his herds, the *possessions* he had gained in foreign lands.) He got off with a dislocated hip (which is bad enough if you think of it under the sign Sagittarius). But he endured and overcame the opposition of the second and the eighth houses, between possession and confrontation with the threatening or abysmal aspect of the deity.

In the eighth house, the challenge is to engage the depths of life. This means experiencing danger, being stretched between the heights and the depths. It is the battle between a force brimming with life (Mars) and the longing for harmony (Venus). And this needs the inflammatory Mars energy, as we saw in Scorpio, to win through to new life or to a more intense level of life. Here the position that Pluto assumes in the process will determine whether the available strengths are raised to a higher power or violated, devoured.

Coming to terms with the questions of death do not always have to run equally vehement courses if signs milder than Scorpio set the tone of the eighth house. But even if at the beginning one likes to think about the goal of the transformative process being demanded, the painful process that leads to transformation cannot itself be circumvented. And the formative background of the eighth house remains the image of Scorpio.

In every instance where the eighth house is emphasized, we find a drive toward intensification of the emotional life. Emotional realities are declared more important than external realities. This will often affect other people as unreasonable, unreliable, indeed threatening. Yet the experiences gained under the aspect of this house can contribute to understanding other persons who undergo crises and feel threatened.

If the sign touches fewer emotional planes, the demand for devotion—or for surrender—shifts toward spiritual depths or toward a fiery social or therapeutic engagement, depending on the element. One turns toward the depths or the needs of others. What one then experiences or "therapizes" in one's counterpart forms a complementary reflection of one's own possibilities.

Ninth House

Old Designation: Pietas *(Piety, Sense of Duty)*
New Designation: Guiding Goals

Already in the eighth house there arose not only the question whether the individual had within a foundation that could carry the load but also another question: What sort of goals did the individual consider possible? Does the individual hold a hope that makes it possible to live? The realm of the ninth house, piety, which stands under Jupiter's aegis in Sagittarius, is completely determined by this question.

Sagittarius not only unites different worlds, Sagittarius lives them in one configuration. The human longing for a union of earthly and divine, for higher goals, for inner freedom, and the hope of attaining this goal create for the ninth house the common denominator piety.

The ninth is opposite the third house. In the third house, we began to become acquainted with the world, acquire bits of knowledge, orient ourselves in space: to the heights, the depths, and the expanses. With Mercury's help in the third house, we can learn to move and express ourselves. The ninth house is concerned with the great journey; in Jungian parlance with individuation; and in religious language with our connection to the divine. We can achieve this only through practice in life and a corresponding inner attitude.

In ancient astrology, this gave rise to the juxtaposition of the third house, to which brothers, siblings, learning, and short journeys were assigned, and the ninth house, to which religion, ethics, philosophy, and great journeys are allotted.

It looks as though the ninth house could build on the third, but there is a great antithesis between the two; they stand in opposition to each other. Whoever in the third house is on the path toward getting to know the world and acquiring knowledge can be so completely absorbed in that endeavor that he forgets the "great journey" and does not even envisage the question of meaning. By contrast, whoever directs his or her energies solely toward goals of the ninth house may, circumstances permitting, consider the acquisition of a body of knowledge, skills, and contacts unimportant. Yet we need experience of life if we are to advance to the question of meaning.

In this arc of tension, agreement can be achieved when Mercury is the messenger but ultimately subordinates himself and remains the mediator, and when Jupiter's breadth can create, awaken, and vitalize meaning on various levels. In Jupiter's function, as in the sign Sagittarius, the tendency toward expansion is revealed: the drive to penetrate vital areas, for example, to direct one's attention to social, ethnic, or ethical concerns and to lend one's support to them. In the concrete as well as in the metaphorical sense, one wants to go on journeys, to make breakthroughs, to explode narrow limits.

The quality of the ninth house brings great tensions with it: on the one hand, a multiplicity of impulses to move (rooted in its nature) and, on the other, the ruling tendency directed toward lofty goals. Concretely this schism can find expression in that the longing to attain spiritual or intellectual knowledge mistakenly believes it has found its fulfillment when it undertakes long journeys (to India, for example).

Hence, the realm of the ninth house is sometimes stamped with restlessness and impatience. Tension can ultimately yield to the feeling of exhaustion and disappointment, the feeling of meaninglessness. But with the new strengths of the centaurs, with new impulses and insights, the bow is drawn again, aimed at the next hope, at a goal that unconditionally concerns one, that one feels is absolutely essential.

All questions asked in the ninth house also will always be questions of meaning: Am I living right? Am I living in accord with my task?

What themes and what goals stand in the foreground at a particular time in life will, in part, depend on the sign of the zodiac and the position of the planets, and in part on the level at which we can take up the questions that have arisen.

But however distant the goal may lie, we attain it in ourselves when we penetrate to our meaning.

Tenth House

Old Designation: Honores *(Honors, Recognition)*
New Designation: Public Life

The tenth house is the fourth cardinal house, the angular house in the midheaven (MC). This house has the character of Capricorn and is determined by Saturn's demands.

Here is revealed, publicly, before the eyes of the world, whether and in what ways one masters one's life; how one controls and represents one's abilities. Here, the way one externalizes oneself becomes visible, which is not to be confused with extraversion. In the realm of the tenth house, the effort or, if it is easy, the joy one experiences in presenting oneself before the eyes of others is revealed.

The house is called honors. Each in his or her own way wants to be seen as he or she wishes to be, usually, of course, from the best side. For this the persona is constructed, the "public garment." It can be identical with the professional uniform if one identifies with one's work: as physician, pastor, artist. Each wears his or her mask, and sometimes there are a number to chose from when one moves in various circles.

What is especially important to a person how he or she comes into relationship with the environment. The way in which one would like to accrue honor is revealed in the domain of the tenth house, depending on the sign and planets present.

Corresponding to the position of the midday Sun, this takes place in broad daylight: publicly visible and in the full light of one's consciousness. Consciously excluded is what should or must not come to light. If, however, one is not conscious of the persona, the mask, or if one unconsciously identifies with it completely, the excluded parts remain in the shadow and become active as shadow aspects.

Thus, the tenth house forms the opposite pole to the homey, cozy, intimate world of the fourth house, "one's own four walls," whereto one can withdraw and where one can bury oneself; where one can be and show how one really is and how one really feels. How one's self-presentation in the tenth house will turn out depends on the security that the ground of the fourth house provides. One person will see only Saturnine demands or tasks that await; another will see the possibility of making demands or of fulfilling expectations. The one remains a slave, the other becomes master of the situation. According to individual judgment, one will dare various heights, and the vistas will present themselves in correspondingly different ways: as gravelly slopes, as wide expanses, as the scope of duty, as fertile land.

The tenth house will reveal in tangible clarity what one is: whether or not one is in accord with oneself and with one's pretensions. The inner goal one bears within or to which one feels duty-bound will be revealed by the heights and honors for which one strives. In the tenth house the way a person leans into the task of mastering the world is revealed.

Eleventh House

Old Designation: Amici *(Friends, Comrades)*
New Designation: Zeitgeist *(Spirit of the Times)*

The eleventh house corresponds to the sign of Aquarius and to the functions of Saturn and Uranus.

Aquarius, viewed as a standing figure, holds his vessel inclined and pours out a stream of stars, of water. He hands on, transmits, what he has collected. Aquarius likes to give, to share with those of like mind, with friends who are moved by the same ideas, although they may not share the same opinions. Hence the eleventh house is called *amici*, friends.

This poses the distinct counterpart to the fifth house with Leo. Where that domain is the intimate, personal realm in which the issue is spontaneous, creative self-expression in the here and now, in the eleventh house the level of self-assurance and satisfaction is not so great because it is not paired with childlike spontaneity. Doubt and uncertainties within as well as the perception of current events urge to intensive intellectual and spiritual confrontation and coming to terms. One is happy and shares concerns (Saturn) and prospects (Uranus), no longer as the sole master on his turf, but among friends, together with those of like mind. In the eleventh house, these concerns and prospects are directed to the future, toward what is in the process of becoming; to the end that a future will be possible and that it may be bearable, indeed meaningful. Above all, one hopes that it will continue so that the abundance of accrued (spiritual and intellectual) possessions can be handed on.

Here it is a question no longer of the pride of the individual ego (as in the fifth house) but rather of a togetherness: surviving together and escaping together. Shared threat moves people to seek shared solutions. In the sign of the eleventh house, comrades come together who feel themselves, in their various ways, bound together by the common goal; groups form that are united by interests; schools are founded. Pupils become friends, disciples, and supporters.

The doubts about the reliability of the future and also about the value of what has been achieved press anew for reconsideration. A veritable torrent of information pours forth, an abundance of genuine knowledge, depending on the group, the team, and the school.

In the sign of Aquarius, whatever psychological, philosophical, and esoteric possibilities enter the field of vision are gathered in and handed on.

Just as Aquarius feels bound by nothing but places spiritual and intellectual independence above all values, so also under the aspect of the eleventh house no conventional bonds are cultivated among friends and in groups. Feelings are not asked after; rather, the common concern is the essential thing. Intimacy lies in the spiritual–intellectual realm, not in the emotional. In this, values that have been handed down are some times all too easily poured out (with the danger of throwing out the baby with the bath water). New values are sought and often stream in from unexpected quarters.

Wherever threats exist, the wish for new plans awakens. Then the danger is of not doing justice to the reality of the present but rather of "lifting off" into unrealistic worlds, either out of skepticism toward the old (Saturn) or through extreme new goals (Uranus).

Having friends can also mean having relationships: patrons or benefactors. And in this there is likewise the demand to further others, to support them on their path into the future. In this sense, one passes on to "spiritual children"—not, as in the fifth house, to real ones.

The signs and the planets in the eleventh house show the form in which the individual will think about the future and make friends with the present. For each of us can only hand on what he or she has or has become as a person in accordance with the signs and planets.

Twelfth House

Old Designation: Inimici *(Enemies)*
New Designation: Anonymity (Private Life)

The name of the twelfth house shows that it is not easy to understand this house correctly and the theme it poses, let alone live it right. Enemies? In the sign Pisces? And of Jupiter and Neptune?

In the opposite house of work, determined by the sign Virgo, it was especially a question of protecting and preserving oneself and of managing, husbanding, providing for, and apportioning in keeping with one's own strengths.

Here, in the twelfth house, which has Piscean character, the demand is the opposite: to yield, get in step with, and plunge into a greater whole—a religious community, a great task, an undertaking beneficial to the commonweal, a political idea or social institution. Difficulties can arise when the surrender of the ego is not successful or finds no recognition so that it is then in danger of being mistaken for ego weakness or a lack of autonomy.

Above and beyond this, there is probably no other house in which it is so difficult to bring about, on the one hand, an agreement between the demands of the area of life constellated and, on the other, planets or signs of another nature that can be positioned in this house. Thus, we can well imagine how difficult the qualities of a Mars in Leo will be when they must be given form precisely in the twelfth house.

The "enemies" that sow discord arise quite early, right in one's own heart: "I want to, but I shouldn't." "Thou shalt not want to have or achieve or accomplish anything for yourself."

Wrongly understood passion brings discord and enmity between one's own talents and those goals that do not let themselves be united with the innate potentials. One becomes one's own enemy because one cannot accept one's own structure. And every counterpart, every colleague, can potentially become an enemy because one does not feel oneself a match for the other. We (Neptune in us) see enemies on all sides who want to devour us; they get in the way of career, or they transgress, disregarding personal boundaries.

It is society or institutions that we often then experience as protective. If the individual can find this sort of shelter and meaningful tasks to which he can completely devote himself (Jupiter's domain), the area of life circumscribed by the twelfth house will be lived harmoniously and in accord with oneself.

The difficult task the individual encounters in the twelfth house lies in being able to surrender the ego for the sake of a greater meaning. Whoever has no ego to defend fears nothing and also knows no enemies. In this way, Paul ultimately succeeded in saying, "Now not I, but Christ liveth in me." Jung called the path of individuation the "path from ego to Self," from the subjectivism where ego is emphasized to the acknowledgment of the suprapersonal authority of the Self.

So here we finally meet with the same goal that already presented itself in the ninth house, likewise under Jupiter's rulership. It lay in the heights and the distance in the sign Sagittarius. In the sign of Pisces, it lies in the depths of the sea. And if we reach it, it lies in our own hearts.

The first time through, we followed the circle of the signs of the zodiac; the second time, the circle of the houses. It remains for the reader to ponder how the various areas of life that the houses outline will take shape when they are "occupied" by other signs than those that determine their respective essence.

In the description of the first six houses, I occasionally suggested how their character, while retaining the same tasks and areas of life, would be modified when signs other than those belonging to them set the tone. The differentiation of the upper six houses is even more complex because ever more "external" possibilities arise for actualizing the individual themes. For each house, for example, actualization is possible in various social arenas. All the helping professions, for example, can be seen both in the meaning of the eighth and as the goal of the ninth houses and offer possibilities for self-actualization in the public life of the tenth, for tasks of the twelfth, as well as for the future-directed plans of the eleventh house.

By and large, I have avoided concrete references to professions, life situations, etc. As I pointed out in the forward, it is not my intention here to present astrological interpretations in detail, but to attempt to impart a fundamental understanding of astrology. The individual horoscope, of course, presents strongly accentuated segments of the totality of possibilities; yet in every horoscope, the entirety of all existing possibilities are also always present. Independent of the individual horoscope, every human being has all the patterns of emotional reaction as they are captured in the various signs of the zodiac more or less distinctly defined at his or her disposal, just as each person is confronted, to a greater or lesser extent, with all areas of life that manifest in the houses.

IV

Quadrants
Elements
Pairs of Opposites
Aspects

Opposition of the Twelve Signs of the Zodiac, 1624

We traced the Sun's apparent annual course through the twelve signs of the ecliptic. The four cardinal points of equinoxes and solstices gave us the four quarters and the four seasons embracing three months each.

Correspondingly, with the division into houses, there arose the distribution into four quadrants that are determined by the apparent daily course of the Sun, by the Sun's position at sunrise, midday, sunset, and midnight. These quadrants are subdivided into three houses each, which are not, however, of equal size and are not congruent with the zodiacal signs but rather usually cut across them.

Analogies exist between the symbolic contents of the signs and that of the houses: the twelve houses correspond to the twelve signs, even if they are not congruent with each other in the horoscope.

The division of signs as well as houses into three sections per quarter or quadrant gives rise to a sequence which we could designate as thesis, antitheses, and synthesis. Older astrology speaks of *rajas*, *tamas*, and *sattwa* houses, or of cardinal, fixed, and mutable.

Quadrants

Each cardinal or angular point in the quadrant corresponds, in content, to a cardinal sign of the zodiac with which a new quarter begins. The following sign—and house—presents a kind of answer, or a counterweight; in the next house, a working through or synthesis of the preceding tendencies is attempted. I referred to this when considering the signs of the zodiac. In the case of the houses, the task of processing or of understanding the cardinal and subsequent house in the final house of the quadrant is revealed perhaps even more clearly.

In the lower half of the horoscope, the third and the sixth houses are ruled by Mercury; in the upper half, thanks to Jupiter, the meaning of the ninth and twelfth houses are more deeply conceived or postulated as task and goal of life.

If in the first house, the ego leaps into life ♈—♂ then in the second the basis for life is sought and taken possession of ♉—♀.

In the third house, knowledge is amassed; one gets to know oneself and acquires the skills of expressing and delimiting one's uniqueness: ♊—☿.

In the fourth house, one seeks relationship to the depths, to the roots or the realms out of which one has grown and by which one was shaped. Here, one can become conscious of how unconscious one is; one finds oneself caught up in a process of psychic growth of which one knows neither when it began nor when it will end. The image of the Moon reflects the phaselike possibilities of development and the relationship to "the feminine," to the yin principle in us: ♋—☽.

In the fifth house, the goal-directedness of the "masculine" or yang principle in us is differentiated out. Here, the need arises to free oneself from the cyclical repetitions and to engage one's own will and strength creatively, uniquely, as a conscious ego: ♌—☉.

The necessity of uniting opposed principles arises now in the sixth house: feminine gathering and masculine sorting ultimately lead to questioning how healthy or whole one's way of life is, how whole one is oneself, and whether one succeeds, even in daily life which is determined by work, in making room for both principles, in oneself and vis-à-vis each other: ♍—☿.

178

Each house of the upper half of the horoscope has the task of replying to the opposite house in the lower half or of mastering and surmounting the task posed there.

The cardinal seventh house begins with the response to a Thou, and as a Thou this is supposed to lead to a proper complement and completion of the I: ♎—♀.

There follows in the eighth house a fierce confrontation and coming to terms with inner and outer conflicts that arise through the obligation to surrender, to give up claims or possessions: ♏—♂—♇.

In the ninth house, one is compelled to subordinate the demands of one's fellows and the knowledge of one's station in the larger context of things to new goals that grant one a presentiment of the supraordinate meaning: ♐—♃.

The fourth cardinal house, the tenth, shows the individual his or her possibilities and the tasks to be faced in mastering the life themes that have been recognized: ♑—♄.

The eleventh house opposes this: not what the individual has attained but what he contemplates with "friends," with or for others, directed toward the future, becomes the task here: ♒—♄—♅.

Finally, in the twelfth house, the demand is to relinquish definitively all egotistical goals. Personal interests, regarded as petty in the face of the total context, are to be placed in the service of a supraordinate, meaningful task.

Ultimately all efforts must flow into the knowledge that each individual is only a minute part (a fish) in the multiplicity of life. Each of us can, indeed, see ourself as the representative of all, but only if we know that we are in the good care of a total context. Joining in this task is possible only when we have at least a premonition of the underlying meaning. But again and again all of us face the struggle for meaning and the battle with doubt, with the "enemies": ♓—♃—♆.

Elements

Aside from the four quadrants with three houses each that follow one upon another in the sense of thesis, antithesis, and synthesis, the four elements are of significance in astrological considerations. They are decisive for the way in which the individual themes presented by the houses can be experienced concretely.

Fire, earth, air, and water correspond to various psychic attitudes or typical forms of experiencing (comparable to the psychological types). But they cannot simply be translated into four psychological terms. Each element is given in three different signs of the zodiac and modified or modulated in three variants. Moreover, it will manifest differently depending on the planets with which it appears and how it is codetermined by the function of the planets.

For example, attempts at translation, such as "mental," "intellectual," "spiritual" or "emotional," "feeling-toned," "empathetic" for air and water, respectively, are inadequate. The elements are to be understood as astrological symbols and cannot be completely grasped by paraphrasing other concepts but rather, at most, can be interpreted by way of hints and allusions.

The element of **fire** is in:	*Aries* ♈
	Leo ♌
	Sagittarius ♐
The element of **earth** is in:	*Taurus* ♉
	Virgo ♍
	Capricorn ♑
The element of **air** is in:	*Gemini* ♊
	Libra ♎
	Aquarius ♒
The element of **water** is in:	*Cancer* ♋
	Scorpio ♏
	Pisces ♓

Each element is represented in three forms and, moreover, each in a specific house: once in a cardinal (C) house, once in a fixed (F) house, and once in a mutable (M) house.

Once again this produces, as previously for the quadrants, a sequence of thesis, antithesis, and synthesis; or of demand, response, and dialogue; and thus, an extraordinary variability of the individual elements.

	Demand **C**	Response **F**	Dialogue **M**
Fire	♈	♌	♐
Earth	♑	♉	♍
Air	♎	♒	♊
Water	♋	♏	♓

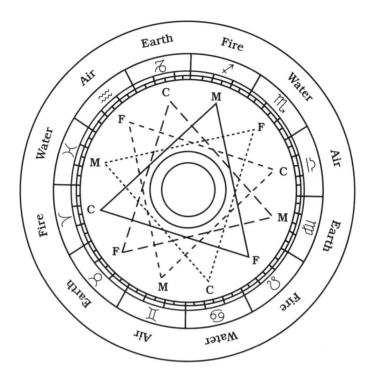

We see how yet again a strong dynamic arises among the signs due to the differing expression of the elements.

In comparison with the almost limitless variety of the possible influences of the quadrants, houses, signs, elements, planets, and their diverse interplay in an individual horoscope, the various psychological types appear one-dimensional and schematic, something of which their originators were fully aware.

Pairs of Opposites

When we considered the signs of the zodiac we encountered yet another energy principle: the sequence of masculine and feminine, of yang qualities and yin qualities, in a consistent rhythm.

These pairs of opposites have to do with the rhythm of tensing and relaxing, a dynamic that presses forward. One principle demands its counterprinciple and again brings about the following principle.

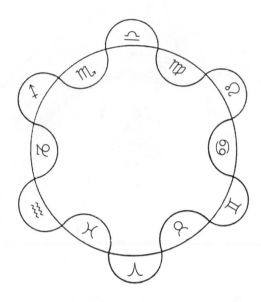

This dynamic can also be described as a tension of masculine–feminine, hard–soft, bright–dark.

Precisely in the context of this sort of dynamic process it becomes clear again that no value judgments are associated with the terms *masculine* and *feminine*, but rather merely complementary parts or aspects of a whole.

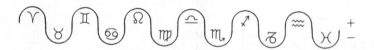

If doubts still linger, assigning the planets to the signs will completely dissolve them, for, aside from the Sun and Moon which represent the essence of the two principles yang and yin, all planets are assigned to two signs, one in a more active and one in a more passive form, corresponding to the yang and yin principles.

Even Mars, as we have seen, can be "passive," that is, can suffer, can be handed over to forces beyond his control, as the myth reports. Venus can be active, full of initiative, and Mercury naturally is present in both realms, and so on.

A horoscope is not a simple diagram; in its unpretentious external form, it contains an abundance of contents that are in-

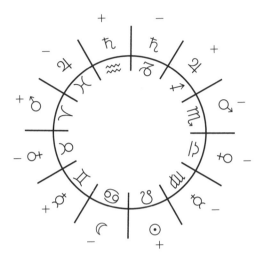

terlinked and interwoven on many levels. The more relations become visible, the more we can sense the dynamic structure and multiplicity of levels of the psyche which exists yet again in each individual in a new configuration.

Aspects

What has been alluded to many times but not expressly included in our considerations are the aspects. Aspects are angular relationships that arise when we sight various planets from our vantage point and connect them with imaginary straight lines.

On each side of such an angle stands a planet that forms an aspect of 90°, 120°, 60° (i.e., a square, a trine, a sextile, etc.) corresponding to the angle.

Two planets apparently in line are in *conjunction*; for the observer, they coincide, even if they are not equidistant from the Earth. Two planets forming an angle of 180° (e.g., one on the eastern and one on the western horizon) are in *opposition*. If the angle formed by two planets is 90°, the planets are square, like the two endpoints of a quadrangle inscribed in a circle. Thus, two planets that we see 120° apart form a trine at the corners of an equilateral triangle inscribed in a circle.

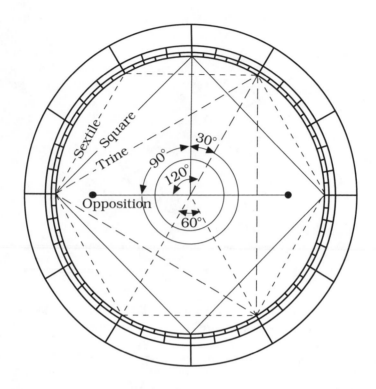

From ancient times only certain angles have been regarded as "effective." They had to correspond to certain numerical relationships for which human beings possess the corresponding geometric instinct—just as humans can hear only tones of certain wavelengths.

The most important aspects are conjunction ☌, opposition ☍, square □, trine △, and sextile ✶; weaker or "minor" aspects include the semisquare (45°) ∟, semisextile (30°) ⩘, sesquisquare (135°) ⊡, and the quincunx (150°) ⚻. Further subdivisions of the circle are possible; but the smaller the angles are, the greater the danger of losing oneself in speculation.

We cannot ascribe any clearly circumscribed meaning to the aspects. Even the designation "harmonious" (in the case of trines) and "unharmonious" (when the circle is quadrated) are misleading. We come closer to their meaning if, following the energy principle, we think of tension and relaxation. Square and opposition are aspects of tension; trine and sextile are relaxed aspects, for here the planetary energies flow together easily. Two energies are mingled in the conjunction. It depends on the individual planetary energies whether their mingling or confluence will be experienced as helpful or not. Relaxed or harmonious aspects are easier to accept. The tension-laden aspects bring with them more difficult tasks, unrest, but also tension in the sense of dynamism in the experiential domain.

Planets that are linked in trine precisely 120° apart share the same element and are already bound to each other.[31] The two energies will find their way to each other, creating reinforcement or mutual support. A sextile (half a trine) is similar to this, but in weakened form.

Planets standing in opposition to each other are two energies with opposing claims, as we learned in the instance of polar signs of the zodiac or houses. We can also imagine two planets as opponents: if they share a context, such as sport (tennis, for example), they can measure their strengths, each to his own advantage. As long as the play continues, they have an eye on each other, they "play ball with each other." As soon as they lose sight of each other, their powers pour off toward completely opposed areas; then each works alone and, under some conditions, one powerfully against the other.

It is otherwise with the square. Here two energies are in tension; they strive apart; they cannot or will not see each other (around the corner). They attack each other from behind and disturb, pester, and aggravate one another. What we cannot see is unconscious; we are unconsciously handed over to the tension. These aspects demand special attentiveness: through repeated "disturbances," inhibitions, incidents, obstacles, we must ultimately pay attention to them and acknowledge them as two energies striving apart that repeatedly stretch to the breaking point the person shaped by them. If we realize them, we sharpen our ability to see them and learn to include them before they attack us. Tension aspects challenge us to a special degree to become conscious.

Aspects point to the dynamic play of the soul and let us conjecture which patterns of experience can more easily become conscious and which will tend more to withdraw from conscious engagement. This dynamic is innate in the individual, present before the outer world presses one into a specific problem.

We can run up against our archetypal structures through typical repetitions such as are mirrored in the horoscope and learn to accept them as belonging to our essential nature.

Conclusion

Our basic structure is inherent in us from the moment of birth, and yet throughout our entire life right up to the moment of our death, our task is to become and to bring to fulfillment what we have been from the beginning.

In the human being—as in every organism—there exists an entelechy: it already contains in itself its fulfillment as a goal (telos). The entelechy is the formative power that rules the development of the organism and the processes in it in a unified, goal-directed way.

It is a most essential part of the dynamic that the two poles, yin and yang, consciousness and the unconscious, condition us and urge us onward. A life path that we traverse consciously (Jung called it the process of individuation) will arise out of the synthesis of conscious and unconscious personality elements. It is a question of bringing together both sides, not of canceling them out in the sense that everything still unconscious must or could be made conscious. On the contrary: it is precisely the horoscope that shows our share of the various realms.

The horoscope can make us conscious of our personal structures, innate potentials, and possibilities. It challenges us to come to terms with aspects of our psyche that have been repressed or never seen and that lead a shadowy existence; to come to terms with parts of our personal unconscious. Beyond that, it shows the individual's share of collectively recognized patterns of experiencing, which have been codified in the astrological symbols. These symbols, on the one hand, represent the collective conscious of humanity; on the other hand, they contain the formative primordial patterns of human forms of experiencing that precondition all experience, the archetypes of the collective unconscious.

Initially, we experience the a priori existing "potential for wholeness" (Jung) reflected by the horoscope in the course of our life process partially, in its individual aspects; only gradually are we able to attain a synthesis of the various parts. Through the process of life, the original, potential wholeness must first become actual wholeness and completeness, in the sense of the old saying: "Become who you are."

Notes

1. Jung wrote, in 1950: "It is remarkable that both sciences, the psychology of the unconscious as well as atomic physics, arrive at concepts that agree in a unique way. . . . [We] conclude that the unconscious psyche likewise exists in a space-time continuum in which time is not longer time and space is no longer space. Correspondingly, causality also ceases to operate there. Physics runs up against the same limit" (1972, p. 177).
2. See, for example, Duerr (1986), Heisenberg (1984), Kakuska (1984), and Capra (1976).
3. On the basis of harmonics, the so-called "octave operations," Kepler arrived at the third law of planetary motion; likewise he (re)discovered the harmony of the spheres, a large number of musical harmonies that result from the course of the planets, their velocity, and distances from one another.
4. "The vital capacity of man contains not only the harmonies peculiar to the rays of the stars but also those inherent in the phenomena of sound itself. Man's vital capacity drinks in the tones with ears like an object that belongs to them. But it takes in the radiations of the stars not with the eyes but rather by means of that dark way and means of knowing described above, and it tests them against the ideas of harmony related to them. For that which offers itself to the eyes serves discursive knowing; but knowledge of the harmonies comes to pass without conceptualization" (Strauss and Strauss-Kloebe 1981, p. 191).
5. "There were many places where Zeus was born, many places where Athena entered the world. . . . Whoever believes he must find contradictions in this that might perhaps be explained by the notion that the Greeks could not agree on the 'true' place . . . has completely misunderstood the essence of mythic space" (Huebner 1985, p. 309).
6. Unless the sources are specifically cited, the following accounts of the Greek myths are based on Kerenyi (1951), Burkert (1977), Lurker (1984), Ranke-Graves (1960), Schadewaldt (1956), and W. F. Otto (1961).
7. The goddesses of fate are the Moirai, "the apportioners," "to whom Zeus of the counsels gave the highest position . . . they distribute to mortal people what people have, for good and for evil" (*Theogony* 904, 906). The goddesses of growth are the Horae: good order, law, and peace. The graces are three and "with fair cheeks . . . from the glancing of their lidded eyes bewildering love distills" (*Theogony* 908–911).
8. According to Hesiod, Hephaestus was conceived and born by Hera alone. Despite this, Hera did not love him; rather, because of his ugliness, she flung him from Olympus, after which he was also lame. But he remained entirely a mother's son, Saturn's heir: with his great skill, he sought to bind Venus and keep her bound.
9. "Conjunction" means "glowing together." In the lower conjunctions, Venus is in Earth's proximity, between the Sun and Earth; its glow coalesces with that of the Sun, that is, Venus is not visible ("new Venus").
10. Maia is the daughter of Atlas, a granddaughter of the Titan, Oceanus. Leto, the mother of Apollo (the older brother of Hermes) is therefore "higher in rank," like Hera.

11. That the word for moon is of masculine gender in German comes from the Germanic root, *me* "to measure," an activity corresponding to the masculine spirit. The moon served as the basis for measuring time. But in Old High German there also existed a feminine form, *manin*, in addition to the masculine form, *mano*; in Middle High German, in addition to the masculine, *mane*, there was the feminine, *moenin*. In ancient languages, luminescence (Selene/*selas* and Luna/*lunare*) rather than measuring was the focus, and the moon was experienced as feminine. But feminine gender of the word *moon* suits both luminescence and measurement, to which the female cycle and the measurement of growth correspond (Kluge 1975).

12. A similarly cyclical feast in Christianity is Easter. Every Easter celebration begins with a shout of joy: Christ is risen! Easter is also associated with the moon: the Resurrection is celebrated on the Sunday after the first full moon of spring.

13. The force or power that produces this effect cannot be comprehended in the horoscope. In Jungian parlance, this would be the Self, the archetype that structures all others in their interconnections and "guides" them; in religious language we might call it God. In the natal horoscope, we can best imagine the Self in the center of the picture, in the empty midpoint of the total energy field or of the whole psychic structure.

14. I will confine myself to observations made in the northern hemisphere in the middle latitudes and which have led to the corresponding astrological statements. Further, I will refer only to the current designations of the constellations and signs of the zodiac, not to their origin or earlier combinations of stars and names.

15. The heavens rotate 366 times around the Earth while the Sun cycles only 365 times. Hence, solar and sidereal times are not synchronous. (For the sake of simplicity, I will describe the movements of the heavenly bodies as they appear to us.)

16. Today we know about 5,000 stars that we can see with the naked eye; medium-strength field glasses reveal some 50,000 to 60,000. The total number of stars that can be seen in photographs taken by the largest instruments on Earth is some 10 billion, but even this number represents only a vanishingly small proportion of the total of all stars in the universe.

17. The Greek *ekleipsis* means "darkness." Only in this plane can Sun, Moon, and Earth lie in a straight line, and only because of this is it possible to have the phenomena of solar and lunar eclipses.

18. During the day, of course, we cannot see the constellations behind the Sun, since the Sun shines too brightly. But by calculating the movement of the stars that we can observe at night, we know what constellations "stand" behind the Sun in the diurnal sky.

19. Compared to the fixed stars, the distance to the planets is quite small: Mercury is 36 million miles from the Sun; Earth is 93 million miles from the Sun; Venus is 67 million miles from the Sun; and Mars is 142 million miles from the Sun.

20. As we recall, the seasons are determined by the inclination of the Earth's axis. The northern or southern hemisphere inclines toward the Sun and experiences the more intense incidence of light, respectively, and thus greater warmth.
21. The objection justly raised against Brehm that he anthropomorphized animal life excessively can only suit our purposes in this context: we are concerned precisely with what humankind projects onto animals—as also onto the stars.
22. An illustrated manuscript from Carolingian times still unequivocally links this set of twins with the constellation Gemini.
23. "Highest elevation" means, for example, that at 50° longitude, the Sun would be directly at the zenith at noon. Our observation that the signs of the zodiac have nothing to do with the effective force of the fixed stars is very noticeable in the case of Cancer. The constellation is especially unimpressive since it contains no bright stars at all but is rather only a loose collection of about five hundred smaller stars distributed over an area three times the diameter of the moon. This is why the ancient Greeks simply called it "fog" or *nephele*, "cloud," until
    they "recognized" in these stars the constellation of the crab, Cancer.
24. Hera (Juno) provided the name for the month of the solstice, June, as Mars did for March.
25. In order to avoid the wrath of Rhea, his wife, Saturn approached the nymph Philyra in the shape of a stallion and sired the centaur Chiron.
26. The first letters of Jesus Christ, God's Son, Redeemer yield the word *ichths*, "fish."
27. Not all the planets in the horoscope stand in the sign of the fishes, Pisces; rather, they are presumably distributed among the other signs of the zodiac. This gives rise to counterforces that lead to a dynamic of various confrontations.
28. To our way of scientific thinking, these sorts of assignments may appear absurd because they cannot be verified by the means available to the natural sciences. We are more inclined to point to human suggestibility. But if we call to mind Chinese medicine, which came to our attention through acupuncture and acupressure, we can convince ourselves that there exist relationships even among various organ systems of the body that we have not been able to perceive from the point of view of our natural sciences.
29. To remain in the realm of symbolic expression, I continue to use the term *houses*, which has been current since antiquity. The concept of "fields" is easily misunderstood as a term from the natural sciences in the sense of physical realities.
30. When additional signs are represented in the house (it can be larger than 30°), they also determine how this area of life is experienced, especially when planets are in these additional signs. But the sign in which the house *begins* sets the tone.
31. We also include as aspects those relationships that are not precise to the degree but that occur within a certain "orb" (i.e., a spherical space of variable size surrounding a planet).

Bibliography

Adler, O. 1950. *Das Testament der Astrologie. Einführung in die Astrologie als Geheimwissenschaft, vol. 1, Die allgemeine Grundlegung der Astrologie—Tierkreis und Mensch.* Vienna.

Barz, H. 1979. *Vom Wesen der Seele.* Stuttgart.

Boll, F., C. Gezold, and W. Gundel. 1977. *Sternglaube und Sterndeutung: Die Geschichte und das Wesen der Astrologie.* Darmstadt.

Borchardt, W., trans. 1924. *Altionische Goetterlieder unter den Namen Homers.* Munich.

_____. 1957. *Gesammelte Werke in Einzelbänden: Gedichte.* Stuttgart.

Brehm, A. E. 1876–1878. *Thierleben,* 12 vols. Hamburg, 1953.

Burkert, W. 1977. *Griechische Religion der archaischen und klassischen Epoche.* Stuttgart.

Capra, F. 1976. *The Tao of Physics.* Boulder, Colo.: Shambhala.

Duerr, H. P., ed. 1986. *Physik und Transzendenz: Die großen Physiker unseres Jahrhunderts über ihre begegnung mit dem Wunderbaren.* Berne.

Freud, S. 1938. Totem and taboo. In *The Basic Writings of Sigmund Freud.* New York: The Modern Library.

Goethe, Johann Wolfgang. 1950. *Sämtliche Gedichte,* vol. 1. Zurich.

Heisenberg, W. 1984. *Physik und Philosophie.* Frankfurt.

Hesiod. *Theogony.* In *Hesiod,* Richmond Lattimore, trans. Ann Arbor, Mich.: University of Michigan Press, 1959.

Hine, D., trans. 1972. *The Homeric Hymns and the Battle of the Frogs and Mice.* New York: Atheneum.

Homer. *The Iliad of Homer.* Richmond Lattimore, trans. Chicago: University of Chicago Press, 1951.

_____. *The Odyssey of Homer: A Modern Translation.* Richmond Lattimore, trans. New York: Harper and Row, 1965.

Hübner, K. 1985. *Die Wahrheit des Mythos.* Munich.

I Ching or Book of Changes, 3rd ed. R. Wilhelm and C. Baynes, trans. Princeton, N.J.: Princeton University Press, 1967.

Jung, C. G. 1948. A psychological approach to the dogma of the Trinity. In *CW* 11:107–198. Princeton, N.J.: Princeton University Press, 1969.

_____. 1952. Synchronicity: An acausal connecting principle. In *CW* 8:417–532. Princeton, N.J.: Princeton University Press, 1969.

_____. 1972. *Briefe,* vols. 1–3. A. Jaffe and G. Adler, eds. Olten und Freiburg.

Kakuska, R., ed. 1984. *Andere Wirklichkeiten: Die neue Konvergenz von Naturwissenschaften und spirituellen Traditionen.* Munich.

Kerenyi, K. 1951. *The Gods of the Greeks.* New York: Thames and Hudson.

Kluge, F. 1975. *Etymologishes Wöterbuch der deutschen Sprache.* Berlin.

Lurker, M. 1984. *Wörterbuch der Symbolik.* Zurich.

Moritz, K. P. n.d. *Götterleherde oder mythologische Dichtungen der Alten.* Bremen.

Otto, W. 1961. *Die Götter Griechenlands: Das Bild des Göttlichen im Spiegel des griechischen Geistes,* 5th ed. Frankfurt.

_____. 1956. *Theophania: Der Geist der altgriechischen Religion.* Hamburg.

Ranke-Graves, R. v. 1960. *Griechische Mythologie: Quellen und Deutung,* 2 vols. Hamburg.

Riemann, F. 1977. *Lebenshilfe Astrologie: Gedanken und Erfahrungen.* Munich.

Ring, T. 1956–1973. *Astrologische Menschenkunde,* 4 vols. Zurich.

Schadewaldt, W. 1956. *Griechische Sternsagen.* Frankfurt.

Sfountouris, A. n.d. *Sternbilder: Blicke in den Nachthimmel.* Zurich.

Strauss, H. A., and S. Strauss-Kloebe. 1981. *Die Astrologie des Johannes Kepler: Eine Auswahl aus seinen Schriften.* Fellbach.

Strauss-Kloebe, S. 1934. Ueber die psychologische Bedeutung des astrologischen Symbols. In *Eranos Jahrbuch 1934.*

_____. 1968. *Kosmische Bedingtheit der Psyche.* Weilheim.

_____. 1984. *Das kosmische Unbewußte in der Persönlichkeit: Geburtskonstellation und Psychodynamik.* Zurich.

Tillich, P. 1964. *Die Frage nach dem Unbedingten.* In *Gesammelte Werke,* vol. 5. Stuttgart.

Xylander, E. v. 1971. *Lehrgang der Astrologie: Die älteste Lehre vom Menschen in heutiger Sicht.* Zurich.